Praise for *Fat,*

'A very honest, funny book. You'll laugh out loud – and shed a tear.'

– David Koch

'This book is "wake up your wife" funny, really funny, screamingly funny.'

– David Vickers, ABC Radio

'As thought-provoking as it is entertaining.'

– *Sunday Herald Sun*

'So brilliant and funny that I neglected my wife and kids for a day so I could read it.'

– *Sun-Herald*

'A thoughtful book that considers modern lifestyle options with measured sensitivity.'

– *Sydney Morning Herald*

'Highly entertaining – offers a frank insight into marriage, family and the gender divide.'

– *Sunday Telegraph*

NIGEL MARSH

Overworked & Underlaid

a seriously funny Guide to Life

ARENA
ALLEN&UNWIN

The lines from 'This Be the Verse' (p. 202) from *Collected Poems*
by Philip Larkin are reproduced courtesy of Faber & Faber

This edition published in 2009

First published as *Observations of a Very Short Man* in 2007

Copyright © Nigel Marsh 2007

Arena Books, an imprint of
Allen & Unwin
83 Alexander Street
Crows Nest NSW 2065
Australia
Phone: (61 2) 8425 0100
Fax: (61 2) 9906 2218
Email: info@allenandunwin.com
Web: www.allenandunwin.com

National Library of Australia
Cataloguing-in-Publication entry:

Marsh, Nigel, 1964-
  Overworked and underlaid : a seriously funny guide to
  life/Nigel Marsh

  ISBN 978 1 74175 659 3 (pbk.)

  Work and family--Australia--Anecdotes.
  Life skills--Australia--Humor.
  Time management.

646.700207

Text design by Darian Causby
Set in 12.5/16.5 pt Adobe Garamond by Bookhouse, Sydney
Printed in Australia by McPherson's Printing Group

10 9 8 7 6 5 4 3 2

Born in 1964 in the UK, Nigel Marsh moved with his family to Australia in 2001. They have lived in Bronte, Sydney, ever since. Nigel's first book, *Fat, Forty and Fired*, has been translated into a number of languages and published around the world. Currently Chief Executive of the communications company Y&R Brands, Nigel is a co-founder of the globally renowned environmental initiative Earth Hour.

Contents

For Kate, Alex, Harry, Grace, Eve...and Mattie

Anthony Robbins

I don't feel that I have the right to tell anyone else what to do – why would I? I'm making it up day to day and muddling through life like everyone else. I do feel, however, that I have the right to be honest regarding what I believe and what I see going on around me. And to be honest I've got a bit of a problem with people who claim to be offering me the 'seven steps to this' or the 'six secrets to that'. As I've got older, I realise I learn more from the people who speak and act gently. Those who don't think they know it all. Much as I love inspirational stories about people who have 'discovered' the secret of happiness or won the Tour de France twenty times, they don't speak to my life. British statesman Lord Salisbury remarked in 1877: 'No lesson seems to be so deeply inculcated by experience of life as that you should never trust experts. If you believe the doctors, nothing is wholesome. If you believe the theologians, nothing is innocent. If you believe the soldiers, nothing is safe.' Not sure I agree with all his examples, but I like his general drift.

Which brings me to Anthony Robbins. If you live in the English-speaking world, the likelihood is that name will ring a bell. Whenever I do a public-speaking engagement, be it in the US, UK or Australia, I always ask, 'Who here has heard of Anthony Robbins?' I'm yet to witness fewer than fifty per cent of hands raised. In most cases, it's nearer ninety-five per cent. Robbins is basically the granddaddy of the motivational world. He is also very tall – six-foot-seven, to be precise. He is to self-help what Picasso is to modern art and Marilyn Monroe is to screen goddesses. His books and tapes sell by the truckload. Someone once estimated that fifty million (yes *million*) people have been to one of his seminars or bought one of his products. I've never met him, but by all accounts he's an impressive chap.

But when anyone mentions Anthony Robbins, I always think of one particular story.

I'm no military historian, but the basic details are as follows. The year was 1880. The country, Afghanistan. A small contingent of troops from the British 66th Foot regiment were marching through the countryside just outside a village called Maiwand. Just as now, a war was being conducted about I don't know what. On this particular date – 27 July – it was destined to be a bad day at the office. Before the British troops had gone barely a mile, they were set upon by thousands of enemy soldiers. An intense and bloody battle ensued. Actually, more of a massacre than a battle. When there was a lull in the fighting after a few hours' combat, there were still thousands of enemy troops left – and eleven British soldiers. Two officers and nine foot soldiers. They were lying in a natural ditch semi-protected by a low wall on one side and a couple of bushes on the other. They were totally surrounded.

Now, the British army has numerous stirring examples of heroism against the odds, and back in Afghanistan in 1880 this tradition was alive and well during the 'Stand of the Last Eleven', as it is known today. The remaining eleven British soldiers had a quick conference and courageously agreed that the best form of defence was attack. In short, they came to the remarkable decision that they were going to *charge* the enemy forces. Right into the heart of their ranks. At the very least, they'd have the element of surprise on their side. Solemn commitments were given that no one would be left stranded. A shot comrade-in-arms would be picked up and carried, if need be. After gathering themselves for the inevitable brutal horror ahead, they let out a collective piercing yell and, to the Afghanis' astonishment, ran headlong into the massed ranks. Guns blazing, half of them full of holes, all eleven of this band of brothers got a full 300 yards. The sun was scorching, they had been fighting all day, they'd just run 300 yards carrying and firing heavy army rifles – they were exhausted. They were now in the middle of thousands of Afghan troops. They stopped running and formed a tight circle, back to back, rifles pointing outwards at the enemy. Then they fired their rifles until every last bullet was gone.

And then the enemy troops killed them.

I tell this story not to mock. In fact, I think it is one of the more poignant stories I've heard. Rather, I tell it because those eleven men had a clear motivating goal, excellent communication, self-belief, high standards, faultless teamwork, positive thinking, proactive urgency – basically, all the self-help golden rules – *and they all died.*

One of the bedrock tenets of the self-help movement is summed up in the phrase 'there is no such thing as failure, only feedback'. Ummm . . . not so sure any of the Last Eleven would describe their grisly end as 'feedback'.

Anthony Robbins himself writes, 'The only limit to your impact is your imagination and commitment.' Again, love your work, Ant, but not so sure.

Of course, I'm being unfair – Anthony Robbins has nothing to do with the Stand of the Last Eleven.

But there is a serious point here. I feel the self-help movement grossly oversimplifies the mechanisms of success. Indeed, grossly oversimplifies life, full stop.

Just maybe, if your father is diagnosed with a terminal illness (as mine has been), it is not appropriate advice to imply that imagination and commitment are going to sort things. Or that positive thinking is the answer. Maybe what's more appropriate is loving, supportive and empathetic acceptance of the reality of the situation. We seem to spend far too much time looking for evidence that life is both fair and controllable, when the obvious truth is that life is blatantly neither. Shit happens, as they say.

This is not a charter to simply give up and stop trying to improve your circumstances or the circumstances of those around you. It is instead a plea for some more honesty. I love thinking positively and consistently striving towards a worthwhile goal. I also believe that Robbins and his like have dramatically helped thousands of people to improve their lives. And yet . . . and yet we need to keep a grip on reality else we start believing a whole heap of bollocks that can actually be extremely damaging.

I believe it's potentially disastrous to give ourselves over to experts or gurus completely. It's important to retain your independence of mind. If you think a 'leading authority' is talking bollocks, it's just possible that they are. Irrespective of how successful or eminent someone is, if they are talking crap, it is still crap.

Four years ago I picked up a small card in an AA meeting. It features the famous prayer: 'God grant me the serenity to accept the things I cannot change, the courage to change the things I can and the wisdom to know the difference.' I realise it wouldn't help me survive a Maiwand, but to my mind it would be a damn sight more useful than the unrealistic hyping of hope that the self-help movement's rhetoric perpetuates.

Not that I'm criticising Anthony Robbins, mind you. Think of the above as merely 'feedback'.

*

My intention here is not to write yet another self-help book. Instead, I would simply like to share some observations I've made. I've learnt a number of valuable (and sometimes painful) personal lessons about change, relationships, parenting, work–life balance, communication and happiness. I don't offer them as answers. I recount them in the humble hope that at best they may be useful prompts for reflection or discussion – and at worst they may provide entertaining solace for people struggling with the same issues that I have struggled with, and continue to struggle with. Certain motivational books can unwittingly make you feel bad about yourself – especially if deep down you suspect you're never actually going to win the Tour de France or awaken the giant within. It's my sincere wish that what follows makes you feel normal and more okay about yourself. If it does, it won't make me an expert but it will make me happy.

Vertically Challenged

In my dream, I was being hit repeatedly on the end of my rather large nose. As the beating continued, it gradually became apparent that I actually *was* being hit on the end of my nose. And that it was still rather large. As I raised my arms to defend myself and prised open my eyes, I saw that the perpetrator of this irritating and painful crime was my younger son, Harry – and that it was 5:15 in the morning. He had been hitting me with what looked like a piece of sparkly cardboard.

'Daddy! Daddy! Wake up! It's Father's Day, and I've made you a card!'

Harry is eight and, with my other three children, Alex, eleven, and our six-year-old identical twins, Grace and Eve, he goes to the local public school around the corner from where we live in Sydney. It's a lovely place and the staff do a great job with the pitiful amount of money the government gives them each year. The parents tend to be quite involved, which gives it an important role in the community and a friendly feel. One of the many cute things they do each year is ask the younger kids to make a card for their dads for Father's Day. When I say 'make', what I mean is that the school pre-makes a card for the kids to complete. It's basically a laminated piece of paper with a wiggly black border and the words 'My Daddy is . . .' printed at the top. The children finish the sentence with a heart-warming message like 'my hero', 'my best friend' or 'full of hugs and cuddles' in the space below and take it home to give Dad on the day itself.

Hence the rude awakening I was receiving on this particular morning.

After a momentary pause, I dragged myself up. 'Made me a card have you, sweetheart? That's lovely of you. Come here and show your old dad.'

I pulled Harry up into the bed next to me and rubbed my eyes, looking at the little mite before reading the words written on the bit of card. Harry is always so cute in the mornings. Hair sticking up, big alert blue eyes, invariably he is wearing one of my running tops inside out, all of which are far too big for him. This morning was no exception – he looked like one of those olden-day kids you see in films, wearing a nightshirt. Despite my weariness, a huge smile spread across my face.

I put my arm around him, gave him a kiss on his forehead and turned to read.

'My Daddy is . . .' went the headline.

Then underneath, in Harry's big, wobbly handwriting, were the words '. . . a very short man'.

There was nothing else on the card. Either side.

Harry was looking up at me expectantly.

'Err . . . That's wonderful, mate . . . Thanks so much,' I said.

'No worries, Dad. Luv ya,' he replied before bouncing out of the bed and rushing downstairs to the sitting room to turn on the TV far too loudly. The jarring sound-track to the Japanese cartoon completed my waking-up process.

Thing is, the little bugger wasn't trying to be funny or cruel. It genuinely was the first thing he could think of to complete the sentence.

I'm not sure five-foot-seven qualifies as 'very' short, but then again, to be fair to Harry, I'm pretty certain it doesn't fit within the tall quadrant, either. It's as if my height is the perfect analogy for the rest of my life – neither tall nor short, neither poor nor rich, neither clever nor stupid. Just an average bloke, plodding along.

And while I might have wanted Harry to write a more flattering description on his Father's Day card, at least he didn't write 'My dad is a rudderless, drunk, out of work, overweight, absent parent' or 'My dad is a self-obsessed tosser who has forgotten what is really important in life and instead dedicates every waking hour to a job he no longer enjoys so he can buy things he doesn't want, to impress people he doesn't like.' Admittedly, descriptions like these would have been a bit of a mouthful for an eight-year-old, but at one time they would have had more than an element of truth to them.

Not that I ever wanted to fit either of those descriptions. But after twenty years on the corporate treadmill as a mortgage slave, I had well and truly lost my way. I just woke up one day and realised that a decade or so of small compromises and put-off dreams had led me to a place I didn't want to be. Basically I had turned into that classic corporate warrior – eating too much, drinking too much, working too hard and neglecting my family. Just to top things off nicely, at the time I was coming to this painful realisation, I lost my job. Not a good Marsh family Christmas that year.

It might have spoilt Christmas, but it turned out to be exactly the kick up the arse I needed. You see, in the middle of this period of self-pity, humiliation and terror, I turned forty – and on my fortieth birthday, I had an epiphany. I suddenly realised that most of the men I knew – in particular, businessmen – talked rubbish. All the time. About everything. To everyone.

To my horror, I realised that I was one of them. This meant that my wife, my boss, my mates, colleagues, children, employees and customers never got the real man they were dealing with. Instead, they got the pretend man.

I suspect many people find it hard to identify their true feelings, let alone express them. In some ways, it's easier to skim along the emotional surface and play out the conventional role that society is happy for you to occupy. Even if every now and then you wake up wondering 'is this it?', it's just somehow simpler to ignore the little voice inside you and carry on as before. Work, earn money, buy things. Work earn money buy things.

Workearnmoneybuythings. Everyone else seems to be on the same conveyor belt, anyway, so it can't be all that wrong. Don't ask why, just earn as much money as you can. Because, after all, the bloke with the most amount of money and toys when he dies wins. Doesn't he?

A pilgrim once asked the fifth-century ascetic St Benedict for advice on how to live his life. St Benedict memorably replied, 'Pause for a moment, you wretched weakling, and take stock of your miserable existence.' Which is precisely what I did a few years ago. I paused. I decided to stop ignoring the little voice inside me. I began, in the words of St Benedict, to 'listen and attend with the ear of my heart'.

After a couple of days of such reflection, I made a promise to myself that I would stop pretending. Stop pretending I believed things I didn't believe and stop pretending I didn't believe things that I did believe. I cut out and put in my wallet these words by eighteenth-century revolutionary Thomas Paine: 'It is necessary to the happiness of man that he be mentally faithful to himself. Infidelity does not consist in believing, or in disbelieving, it consists in professing to believe what he does not believe.'

So rather than look for another job, I decided to take a year off and try to wrestle back some control and purpose into my life. It wasn't all beer and skittles – just ask my wife, Kate; living with a man who is 'finding himself' isn't the best fun in the world – but I did have a modicum of success. I gave up the booze, lost the weight, got respectably fit and, most importantly, connected properly and meaningfully with my family. I also wrote a book called *Fat, Forty and Fired* about that particular period of my life . . . but to cut a long story short, I took a year out from the corporate rat-race to get my house in order.

House in order or not, my finances were quickly rooted. Wonderful though my 'time off' was, I had to return to work sooner rather than later because the savings were rapidly running out and we had no income. Gorgeous as our kids are, they do have to eat and wear clothes. All four of them. Whenever any of those 'are you properly prepared for your retirement?' super ads came on TV, I'd feel physically sick. *Screw my retirement*, I'd think – *I don't know how we're going to get through September*. So when I was offered the job of CEO of the Australian office of an international communications company, I took it.

On my return to the workforce, I suspected that although my new-found, or rediscovered, 'enlightenment' might make me happier, it would probably also make me a 'loser' in the cut and thrust of commerce. It's all well and good getting back in touch with your feelings and family, but tree-hugging ain't going to get you to the top of the career ladder. Still, this was a price I was prepared to pay in my bid to stop living a life I had come to believe was shallow and unauthentic. Turns out I was only half right. It did (and does) make me happier. Bizarrely, though, it also made me more, not less, successful in traditional terms. I thought I'd be less effective in the workplace. Precisely the reverse was the case. I found it easier to make effective decisions without the previous pretence. It seems authenticity makes commercial, not just personal, sense.

However, any notions that a quick-fix one-off break was all I'd needed were soon dispelled. I may have been 'fit, forty-one and hired', but I still had to face the same demons. Juggling what's important with work is a damn sight easier when you haven't got any work. By the same token, no one's going to pay you for being an enlightened SNAG who does the school run each day, either. It was one thing coming to the realisation that I was no longer the man I wanted to be, another to work out the type of man I wanted to be – and yet another thing entirely to be able to follow that aspiration through. In real life. Day to day, here and now.

The playwright Anton Chekhov once said, 'Any idiot can face a crisis – it is day-to-day living that wears you out.' He's got me bang to rights. I've had my crisis. Even dealt with it moderately well, thank you very much. But what about normality? How am I going to deal with that in a way that makes me proud I am living up to my hopes and dreams? I've made a lot of changes in my life in a short period of time, and one thing I've noticed is that any 'improvement' I've made gets significantly more difficult to sustain when what I call the 'wow, haven't you lost lots of weight!' phase is over. In the first few weeks after you've given up drink, it is interesting and worthy of affirmation and support. Four years on, and no one gives a toss. Kicking it all in for a year and living off your savings is all well and good, but it's not a recipe for the next ten, twenty or thirty years.

I want to learn how to live well. Not well in terms of having a yacht, but well in terms of making a positive contribution and leaving the world slightly better than how I found it. On a sustained day-to-day, year-to-year basis – without becoming a sanctimonious, joyless, superior prick.

Thousands of years ago, Socrates maintained that the unexamined life wasn't worth living. I reckon it's a thought that is every bit as relevant today. Why on earth do we live as we do? Why on earth do *I* live as *I* do? What's the point of it all? To my mind, just because you think it's unlikely that you'll ever find the definitive answers doesn't mean you should stop asking the questions.

Reality

When my wife, Kate, read the Father's Day card Harry had made, she remarked with a resigned shrug, 'Being short is the least of your problems, Nigel.'

Now, I may be ordinary but there is one exceptional thing about me and that's my wife. Or, as my friend Todd puts it, 'the best thing about Nigel is Kate'. Thanks, Todd. I met Kate more than twenty years ago, when we worked for the same company in London. To my friends' astonishment and my parents' delight, I somehow talked her into marrying me. Having promised not to get in the way of her already impressive professional progress, I immediately proceeded to get her pregnant three times in quick succession. The fact that the third time was with twins neatly destroyed any remnants of her career. The other promise was to keep her near her family in London. The move to Sydney took care of that one.

Kate's not so good in the mornings, but I could see where she was coming from. Because two years after re-entering the rat race I'd realised that, while I may have been making the best of the situation, perhaps there was a different path. A path where I changed not just the attitude – but the *situation* as well. I've come to believe that balance isn't about having it all – it's about making intelligent choices. Perhaps the answer had been staring me in the face all along and was brutally simple – rather than attempting to be an enlightened office rat, maybe I should simply stop *being* an office rat.

'Fine, in *theory*,' Kate had said when I revealed my grand plan. 'But how do you propose we're going to pay the chuffing mortgage and feed the kids?'

She had a point. Kate usually does. Throughout our marriage, she has been the voice of sense and reason. She doesn't pander to me – a characteristic that on more than one occasion has saved the family from total disaster. Moreover, at the risk of making her sound a saint, she manages at the same time to do a remarkable thing – she combines her regular doses of realism with constant encouragement.

But now, having already put up with one career break that destroyed any savings we had managed to put by, she faced me, and therefore us, doing it all over again. This time without a redundancy payout.

What was worse, from her perspective, was the inconvenient truth that my post-year-off re-entry into the corporate world couldn't have been more triumphant – in the traditional definition. The firm I went back to run had a wonderful period of success – profits up, revenue up, corporate awards coming out of our every orifice. Perfect timing after three years in charge, then, to leverage this success – cash in and take the big job in head office. And what does Nigel want to do? Move to New York and take on the world? Nope, instead he wants to kick in his job and start training for his Bronze Medallion lifesaving qualification. Marvellous – that will pay the bills.

Kate knew that with me committing career suicide for the second time in four years she would yet again be condemned to a life of regular arguments about stupid little things. Like 'Why can't you buy homebrand shampoo instead of the expensive stuff?' or 'Do the kids really need curtains in their bedrooms, anyway?'

Nevertheless, despite her entirely understandable misgivings, last year I once again turned my back on traditional career advancement. I moved into the chairman role at Leo Burnett, the company I work for, and now, rather than spend my days at a desk in an office, I divide my time between family, writing and public speaking. Which basically means I have swapped worrying about having a shallow one-dimensional life for worrying about having enough money to keep our heads above water. I have days when I'm not sure it was such a clever exchange. It's entirely possible I *won't* be able to make the finances work. But I'm sure as hell going to give it a try. Irrespective of how scared and uncertain I am about the future, I'm committed to giving a different, less conventional, path a go. And unlike last time, this time I've *chosen* to step out of the rat-race.

Now, this is a personal, individual choice, and I'm not criticising how other people choose to lead their lives. It's just that I suspect there are many ordinary people who don't actually *choose* their life. It just sort of happens. And actually there's not much wrong with it. But at the same time, as you get older you can start to wonder if maybe there isn't more to life. You are basically a nice person and you're working diligently to look after your family and climb the career ladder, but somehow it all feels a little hollow. A little like you are marching to the beat of someone else's drum. In many ways, I envy those people who have no element of doubt that the next promotion is obviously the thing to go for. I'd love that level of certainty.

In its absence, however much I tried, I simply couldn't stop asking, 'Why?' Why is it better to get richer and more senior? Why do the people in the first-class lounge look so damn miserable? Why is it the right thing to dedicate myself to this firm for the next twenty years until retirement?

I was shocked when I decided to look – really look – at the people 'above' me and discovered that the truth was, although I liked many of them, I couldn't find one whom I *admired* – whose life I coveted.

At this time, I read a wonderful quote from the former White House speech writer Ben Stein, who said, 'The first step to getting the things you want out of life is this: decide what you want.' I've come to believe that you have to take personal responsibility for the type of life you want. The cliché unfortunately *is* true – if you don't design your life, someone else is going to do it for you. And as much as I respect and feel affection for the companies I've worked for, I'd rather *I* planned my life than they did.

Part of making this choice involves learning how to divorce my self-worth from my career or job title. It's clearly something many people simply can't do. To them, your identity is so completely wrapped up in your job title that if you haven't got a job, you haven't got an identity. I cringe when I think of the occasions in the past when I must have been hideously socially awkward by not being able to see past a person's lack of traditional employment. I now have a greater understanding of how challenging it must be for women who make the decision not to go back to their job or career after having kids. Challenging not only when they have to respond to the relentless 'what do you do?' questions but also challenging to their own internal sense of identity and self-worth.

I hate to spoil the dreams of any bored office rat out there, but not going to work every day isn't a problem-free paradise, either. I wouldn't quite agree with my brother's description of my life as 'poverty-stricken domestic tedium', but there is a certain relentless grind to the day-to-day reality of family life that you can't fully appreciate if you're used to knobbing off to the office every day.

One of the biggest lessons this time around, however, is that I can't do it all on my own. Nor should I try. I've had some much-needed humility beaten into me. As the wonderful writer Michael McGirr once said, 'We are enriched by what we can't do, even more by what we choose not to do. The secret of being human is learning how to enjoy our limitations. If we could do everything we wouldn't need other people.'

I need my wife, I need my family and I need my friends. I couldn't do any of the things I want to without them. That's the reality.

I also need some more money, but that's another story . . .

Pizza

I'm deeply aware of my personal flaws (how could I not be – Kate reminds me most mornings), and ever since my mid-life epiphany I've devoted considerable time and effort to making some big changes in my life. I'm happiest when working towards a goal – the bigger, the better. A recent episode with my son Harry, however, helped me realise that big changes aren't necessarily always what's required. Last winter, Kate went on an interstate trip with our two girls at the same time that Alex was away on a rugby tour. Someone needed to pick Harry up from school. It was agreed that on this one day, I would bunk off work early and collect the young lad, feed him and put him to bed.

I made sure I got to the school early enough to see Harry rush out of his classroom when the bell went. After checking he had all his stuff in his blue schoolbag, I walked him to the local park where we messed around for an hour or so – did some races, played some silly games. Then I walked him to the local pizzeria and we shared a pizza for dinner. Next, I gave him a piggyback home, ran him a bath and read him two chapters of Roald Dahl's *James and the Giant Peach* before tucking him up under his Batman doona and giving him a goodnight kiss on his forehead.

As I was leaving his bedroom, he called out, 'Dad.'

'Yes, mate,' I replied.

'Dad – this has been the best night of my life. In real life. Ever,' he said.

I was floored. I hadn't done anything – yet it ranked as the best night of Harry's life.

The moral of this story hit me like a sledgehammer – the small things matter. Really matter. I had spent far too much of my life as a parent worrying about the big things to realise that those everyday, regular, inconsequential actions actually matter just as much, if not more. With respect to the famous author Richard Carlson, '*Do* sweat the small stuff.'

With four young kids, it's so hectic that you can find you never spend one-on-one time with any of them. After Harry's 'best day' remark, I sat down with Kate and we worked out a plan to rectify this. Now, every Tuesday is 'Daddy's afternoon'. Basically, this means that on a rotating basis, I take each of my kids out alone for a trip with Dad after school. We don't do anything flash or expensive – it's just a guaranteed day once a month where they get to spend time alone with Dad. The effect has been magical. The trips have already provided some of our most special memories, as well as doing wonders for the relationship I have with each of them. The most astonishing thing, however, is how huge the return has been for such a little investment. We are, after all, talking about an hour or so a month with each child.

And this got me to thinking. After a month or so of Daddy's afternoons, I started to feel that if this 'small things can make a huge difference' philosophy was true in child-rearing, then maybe, just maybe, it might apply to other areas of life as well.

To take one example, I regularly get asked to talk about the issue of work–life balance. I have strong views on the topic. Like sex, it's one of those areas where everyone seems committed to never revealing their true feelings. But if we are to make any progress as a society towards successfully enabling our citizens to live more balanced lives, the first step has to be forcing ourselves to be honest. I come across so much misleading and blatantly untruthful garbage about the issue, it makes me want to weep.

Certain unpalatable truths need to be faced.

First off are the economic realities – it's all very well boffing on about leading a less work-dominated life if you've got the financial means to do so, but many people have literally no choice other than to work their arses off to survive. If you're on Struggle Street, it's not really an option to do four hours of Pilates in the middle of the day to centre yourself.

Second is the fact that many jobs and careers are inherently going to lead to an unbalanced life. Being a city trader for Macquarie Bank means you won't be home for the kids' dinner – whatever they tell you in the interview. Come to think of it, I'm pretty sure they *do* tell you that in the interview.

Third, for most people, life will go through a variety of stages. For many, this will involve a perfectly natural period when they are completely happy being full-on in their job. If you're young, just starting out and don't have kids, putting your shoulder to the wheel for a few years can be just what the doctor ordered.

Then there are the people who don't want a balanced existence. It's not my personal choice, but different strokes for different folks. Looking after young kids isn't always fun – it can frequently be soul-destroying hell. Boring, thankless and exhausting. Besides, if you want to run the world, spending your afternoons doing the school run is probably not going to cut it.

Add to this the reality that the vast majority of firms don't want truly balanced employees – whatever they say in their ridiculous annual reports. They secretly prefer employees who are 100 per cent committed and put work above all else.

And don't forget the employees who *aren't* parents – they resent having to pick up the slack in the office for those of us with kids. They find your stories of how hard it is juggling work and family boring and irritating. When your child-minder is sick for the tenth time in a calendar year and you have to leave work early to fill in for her, they aren't always thinking 'Oh, poor Amanda, it's a marvel how she copes' – they are more often than not thinking 'Bloody Amanda, she's always bunking off and leaving us in the lurch'.

Beyond the fact that everyone talks rubbish about it, I learnt two things about work–life balance from my year off and the subsequent three years back in the rat-race as a supposedly enlightened CEO. I offer these not as answers – as I said above, the issue is far too complex for one-size-fits-all answers. I offer them as *suggestions* to people like me who need to work but are finding it difficult to remain meaningfully connected to their families on a day-to-day basis.

The first suggestion is to stop thinking of it on a day-to-day basis. I spent an entire year after having gone back beating myself up because I could never seem to be home for the kids' dinner more than two days in a row.

Of course I couldn't. I was the CEO, for Christ's sake. What a bloody stupid goal.

After a year, I surrendered to the inevitable demands of my particular job and, rather than looking for balance in my life on a daily basis, I extended the time frame. I started judging myself by weekly and monthly criteria. The effects were dramatic. It wasn't just more realistic, it was more flexible. It enabled me to pull my weight appropriately when circumstances required. It's not really conducive to staff morale when the rest of the office is gearing itself up to work its collective arse off into the evening for you to gaily announce 'right-oh, I'm off to pick the kids up' at 4:15 in the afternoon.

I began to set myself weekly goals, not daily ones. I'd plan the week ahead and set modest objectives such as taking the kids to school and picking them up *once*, being home for a family dinner *once*, having at least *one* evening out with my wife, etc. I'd deliberately set the bar low so that if I didn't meet my targets, I couldn't wriggle out of my failure by claiming the goals were unrealistic in the first place. I *knew* they were more than reasonable.

Each week, I'd review my progress against my goals. If I failed, I'd simply note that failure and extend the time frame again, saying to myself, 'Be realistic, Nigel, that was week one – give it a full month to see how you go on average.' I'd review progress each week for a month, then look back at the end of each month. I allowed myself to fail over a month as long as I got back on track during the next month. Not made up for the missed commitments but got back on track and met them for that month.

If I failed two months in a row, then I forced myself to conclude that the wheels had come off and I was living my life in a manner that was inconsistent with my self-proclaimed desire to be meaningfully engaged with my family. Lots of short-term realities put back to back become your long-term reality. You can't keep on pushing back the deadline or you'll end up like those sad, deluded fools who claim they are going to reorganise their priorities *when they retire*. Have you ever heard anything so ridiculous?

It's no good waiting until retirement to get some balance and perspective into your life – *you'll have nothing left to balance, you knob jockey*. The whole point is to try to do it as you go. Call me a cynic, but sorting work–life balance when you no longer have any work is hardly a herculean achievement. It's like learning to love your wife after she's divorced you – or appreciating your kids only after they've left home. I haven't got any answers, but I would like to suggest that these skills would be better put to use *before* you stop work – or indeed before your wife and kids leave home – not after.

Extending your time frame for judging yourself in the balance department is my first suggestion. My second is to look at how you define balance in your life.

I've met hundreds of people who are passionately committed to working more balance into their lives yet unwittingly making no difference at all. And never will

– until they change the way they look at what balance means. The reason for their failure (in my eyes) isn't that they aren't genuine in their desire to change. Nor is it that they lack the commitment to follow through on their intentions. It is that they approach balance in a fundamentally *unbalanced* way.

I believe a human life can be divided into four parts – the intellectual, the physical, the emotional and the spiritual. Simplistically, let's equate the intellectual with the world of work. Many people in today's hectic market-driven society believe the intellectual/work part is unreasonably dominating their lives. So what do they do? They join a gym.

Brilliant – that's going to sort it.

I don't mean to mock. It's just horrifying to me to see people who have correctly identified that their lives are unhealthily one-dimensional making matters worse by joining a bloody gym. Nothing wrong with gyms, mind you. It's the logic that being a 'fit fourteen-hour-a-day office slave' is somehow more balanced than being an 'unfit fourteen-hour-a-day office slave' that is wrong. It's not more 'balanced', it's just more . . . 'fit'.

Similarly, it's just as nonsensical to realise that your work is dominating your life and give up work altogether.

As I said earlier, there's a lack of honest debate about this issue. You've got a duty to feed the kids somehow and, apart from the privileged few, you'll always have to work to earn a living to be able to do this. Rather than denying that fact and yearning for some never-to-be-reached future state where you are work-free, better to embrace the fact with open arms and put your energies into looking for work that more closely fits into your value system.

My second suggestion therefore on work–life balance is to attempt to tend to all four areas of your life. It doesn't matter what your particular brand of spirituality is, or how you define your emotional life, or which fitness regimen you subscribe to. Simply start by asking yourself: *am I* doing something *in each of those four areas?* Not 'doing a lot', just 'doing something'.

In my attempts to gain balance, I fell into the fitness trap. I was unhappily working my nuts off in my chosen career and somehow managed to convince myself that if I could only just lose a bit of weight and work a few runs into my routine, then everything would be peachy.

However, my life changed not when I lost a few kilos and ran around the park, but when I was nicer and more considerate to my wife (emotional), and it transformed when I started prioritising one hour a week for quiet contemplation (spiritual). It's just a little too confronting for some – especially men – but forcing yourself to do something in *each* of the four areas of your life can yield astonishing results.

I know that so many men have an in-built resistance to this stuff. I did. *I'd really like to get more in touch with the important things in life, but I can't afford to become a loser just yet. I need to pay the mortgage off before I go and get me some balance.*

I know I'm short, but please trust me on this one – don't wait until your life is 'sorted' till you get some balance.

Instead, get some balance and I believe you might just find it will help you sort your life.

Cooma

From the very first day of my re-entry to the workforce, I was counting down the days till I left it again. I had given my word that I would stick with the new job for three years. I was unshakable in my determination to do just that but equally determined that it wouldn't be one week or even one day more than three years.

Sure enough, on the day of my third anniversary in the post, I said goodbye to my job and my colleagues, drove home and took the family on a skiing holiday to Thredbo. I'd been looking forward to this trip for over a year – both as a holiday but also as a milestone to mark my transition once again from corporate man to family man. Besides, all the kids love the snow, and as I wouldn't be able to afford to take them skiing for a while, given my reduced financial means, Kate and I planned this as the last such holiday for the foreseeable future.

To save money, we'd hired an apartment up the hill a good walk away from the ski lifts. It was nice enough, but 'budget-priced' would probably best describe the location – up four flights of stairs and above a super-market. We were knackered simply walking to the slopes, let alone skiing down them. On the first morning, after the tortuous process of hiring our kit was completed, we proceeded to walk, together as a family, to the bottom of the lifts. Awkward in uncomfortable ski boots, irritated by the shiteness of the inevitable 'first day admin phase' of every skiing holiday, my nerves began to fray as the sibling bickering got noisier and noisier, building to the usual crescendo where one or other of the kids ended up crying. This time it was Eve who collapsed in tears as Grace, her sister, entirely without provocation or warning, hit her hard with her helmet when she was looking the other way while innocently standing in the lift queue.

Kate asked me to mind Alex and Harry so she could take the girls aside and calm them down.

When peace was restored, Kate and the girls returned to the queue and Kate whispered to me, 'Nigel, I've said my piece to them both, but given that it was Grace who started it I want to make sure she in particular learns her lesson. Could you please have a word with her?'

'Sure,' I replied, confident in my role as patriarch.

I wanted to set the tone for an obedient holiday (and indeed obedient rest-of-my-life-as-a-stay-at-home-dad) so I laid it on a bit thick. Towering over my identical twin daughters, who even though I say it myself were looking positively angelic, dressed as they were in matching salopettes and hats, I turned to Grace and, with a serious look in my eyes, said to her in a stern voice, 'Your behaviour is unacceptable. You've let me down. I'm disappointed in you. This is your one and only warning. If you misbehave again, Daddy will take your equipment back to the shop and there'll be no more skiing for you for the whole of the week, young lady. Do YOU UNDERSTAND ME?'

'Yes, Daddy,' she replied in a small, chastened voice before starting to cry.

'Why are you crying?' I snapped.

'Because I'm *Eve*,' she replied.

Brilliant. I'd given up work to spend time with my family and I couldn't even tell my own daughters apart.

When we eventually got on the chairlift and made it to the top of the mountain, the crying had stopped. The anticipation of the skiing ahead and the beauty of the surroundings had wiped out all the previous stress and negativity. The weather was perfect, the snow beautifully groomed, and the slopes beckoned. *I'm not just on holiday*, I thought, *I'm no longer a corporate battery hen*. I wanted to scream with joy.

'Right, last one down is a sissy,' Kate shouted, pointing her skis downhill.

'Unfair start. Mum's a cheat. Get her, kids!' I yelled.

Alex, Harry, Grace and Eve bombed off down the mountain. Kate and I pretended to be going as fast as we could as the kids whizzed in and out between us, whooping and hollering. It was ecstatic, energising bliss.

I couldn't help but count my blessings. At that moment, as I looked at my wife and kids hurtling down a mountain in Thredbo, my heart ached with affection for them. I just couldn't believe that for so long I had arranged my life in such a way as to spend the vast majority of my time away from them.

I was still deep in the middle of this Pollyannaish reverie when we reached the bottom. Alex had won, closely followed by Harry who, unlike any of his siblings, was somehow already covered in snow from head to toe.

My brother describes Harry as 'cherubically naughty' and, looking at my younger son smothered in snow and grinning from ear to ear, I could see how the description was perfectly apt. Grace and Eve had forgotten the helmet incident and were yelling in unison, 'Daddy's a slowcoach! Daddy's a slowcoach!'

'Down again, kids?' Kate asked.

'Yessss!!! Pleeeaaasse!!!' they chorused.

We started to shuffle our skis along the flat ground towards the base of the chairlift. Kate was in front, Harry just behind her. To help him along, she turned and offered to pull him with one of her ski poles. The moment she pulled, she winced and stopped, then went deathly white.

'What's the matter? Are you all right?' I asked.

'My back. I think I've done my back,' she groaned.

'Don't worry. I'll pull Harry. Let's just get you on the chairlift to give it a rest,' I said optimistically.

'No, I *really* think I've done my back. I can't move,' she replied. Now, she looked scared as well as white.

'Don't be silly, sweetheart. It'll be fine,' I said, without any evidence whatsoever to back up my assertion.

Turns out she wasn't fine. We didn't go up the mountain again, either. Instead, we carried her the kilometre or so to our chalet and then agonisingly, slowly and painfully, step by step up the four flights of stairs to our apartment.

'It's getting worse,' Kate said as we laid her on the floor. 'You'll have to call a doctor.'

Now, I've a thing about calling doctors. I always feel guilty using them. I never feel as if I'm *ill enough* to waste their time. Even if I've got a gaping wound the size of a manhole cover in my chest, I'm worried that by the time I get to the doctor it will have healed and I'll look like a time waster.

'Let's just leave it a while to see how it goes,' I said.

To my shame, that is precisely what we did. For five hours, we sat as a family watching Kate scream in agony every time she tried to move, before I eventually called the doctor. When he arrived, he took one look at my wife and immediately called an ambulance.

I tell this story not because of its intrinsic interest but because of my *mental reaction* when the ambulance crew arrived and began to carry Kate down the stairs before driving her to Cooma Hospital. She was clearly in agony. Just hours earlier, I had been musing about how much I loved her and the kids, and how I wanted to focus on being a homemaker, yet my overriding thought now, as she was being put in the ambulance, was not 'Poor Kate!' but 'How am I going to cope with four kids on my own for a week?' quickly followed by 'What a tragic waste of money! We've pissed thousands of dollars up the wall to ski for a week and you're not going to do more than one run the whole holiday!' topped off by 'This is the last skiing holiday we'll have in years and you've gone and bollocksed it up for everyone!'

I'm not proud of my reaction. I'm just being honest about the matter. I wonder how many other people secretly resent their partners when they are blamelessly but inconveniently ill – but don't feel they could ever admit it.

It's one thing being the father of four young kids when you've got a PA, nanny and fit wife to do all the difficult stuff – and when you can run away to the office whenever things get a little too hard. It's another thing entirely when you no longer have any of those and have nowhere to run to in the tough times. Here I was, barely two days into my second 'I want to be a family man' career break, and I couldn't bear the thought of spending the week ahead with them alone. It was enough to give hypocrisy a bad name.

I'm pleased to report that although I generally made a goose of myself for the next five days, with a lot of 'beyond the call of duty' help from good friends, I did cope. I got the kids to the slopes on most days and even managed to get them into bed before midnight on two occasions. Unflattering though this story may be, the week served to remind me of two lessons. First, to marvel again with renewed respect at the incredible unsung job stay-at-home parents do. Second, it provided me with unarguable evidence that I was indeed a wretched weakling who clearly *did* need to pause for a moment and take stock – not only of his miserable existence, but also of his *mindset and priorities*.

I was, after all, setting out on this new chapter of my life to put the things that mattered to me at the centre of my life – not merely to give them a bit more attention but essentially leave them at the edges. Clearly, to do this was going to push me beyond my comfort zone. Equally clearly, if I was to succeed, I was going to have to force myself to retain an open mind . . .

Mattie

Truth be told, though, if I'd known in advance that 'retaining an open mind' would quickly translate into 'getting a bloody dog', I would have probably called off the whole lifestyle transition there and then. It's not that I hate dogs, or dog owners. It's just that I hate the *concept* of dog ownership. Or, more accurately, the concept of *me* getting involved in dog ownership.

So while I don't *hate* dogs, it would be stretching things to say I like them. For forty-odd years, I've been indifferent to the charms of man's supposed best friend, and I'm not that keen on their owners, either. In their own way, each seems as bad as the other. I'm terrified of the beasts, which I admit isn't a good starting point.

They always seem to be looking at me in a suspicious 'if I felt like it, I could rip your throat out' way. Then there's the incessant barking when you come to the door or run past them in the park. Maybe they can smell my fear. The behaviour of their owners on these occasions is almost always of the incredibly irritating 'oh, don't mind Rex, he'd never hurt anyone, his bark is far worse than his bite' variety. *Then why don't you train the thing to shut up*, I can't help thinking. Just because your dog hasn't bitten anyone yet doesn't alter the fact that hundreds of kids are attacked, scarred and in some cases permanently maimed or killed each year by dogs. Dogs that up until that very moment were someone's adored, harmless, 'bark is worse than his bite' poochy-woochy.

You know it's not going to attack me. *I* don't know until you tell me. It's not cute or endearing, it's really antisocial, selfish and thoughtless. If I had a fourteen-year-old son who habitually ran up to strangers waving a knife around and shouting 'aarrggh!!!!' in their faces, and all I could say was 'he finds it funny, but don't worry, he's never actually stabbed anyone', I don't reckon I'd get away with it.

And then there's the shit. Everywhere. Roads, pavements, parks, beaches. They shit everywhere – in staggering quantities. Especially the little ones. It's as if the smaller they are, the bigger their excretions. I often catch myself looking at small dogs and imagining they are really just one huge, fur-covered turd with legs. Most owners make a good show of carrying poo bags, so I can't understand how the world is still smothered in dog shit. The unmistakable smell, and mess, when one of my children has walked all over the house in a trainer that is covered from toe to heel in dog excrement makes me want to vote for the return of capital punishment for minor offences.

Last but not least there's the crutch sniffing, leg shagging and inappropriate mounting that characterises any trip to the park these days. Again, a ditsy dog owner breathlessly running up to you, ineffectually shouting 'down, Shep!', only makes it worse.

So what have I done with this long-standing and deep-seated hatred of the concept of me owning a dog?

Yep, that's right – I've gone and got myself one.

A Jack Russell called Matilda Kylie Alicia Moonbeam Starlight Robbie Husky Marsh. A bit of a mouthful, I know, but we'd promised the twins they could name the bloody thing and made the fatal error of failing to mention that we were only after *one* name. They'd spent hours locked in their room deciding, so when they came out hand in hand, gazed up at us with their huge, trusting blue eyes, and solemnly told Kate and me the poor mutt's intended name, we couldn't face breaking our word – a promise is a promise, and all that. Luckily, three days of shouting her full name in the park convinced even Grace and Eve that an abbreviation or nickname might be in order. Two more hours of locked-door consultation and, to our relief, we were informed that 'Mattie' was to be the shortened version.

It had taken a lot of cajoling to make me crack and get one. I blame the kids. Unlike Kate, we never had a dog in our family when I was growing up, so I've no personal experience of deliriously happy childhood moments with Lassie to remember. From the word go, however, for some reason all of my kids have expressed a passionate desire for a dog. Kate has constantly pestered me to get one, saying the children would adore it – and, as an added bonus, would not end up a dog-fearing wuss like me. Just because I had a screwed-up, dog-bereft childhood, she reasoned, didn't mean I had to inflict one on my children.

I countered with arguments about the expense, the hassle, the fact we could hardly cope looking after four kids, let alone a pet. I told horror stories of laborious late-night walkies when all you wanted to do was flop into bed, long car trips ruined by incessant yapping, unwanted puppies, dog hairs forever ruining the furniture, foul-smelling dog food, restrictions on where we could go on holiday. Everything I dreaded about having a dog and more.

The stories had no effect. Harry started bringing back books from the library with titles such as *The Joy of Dog Ownership* and *How to Care for your Dog*; the girls' school projects all began to have dog themes. One of these (Eve's) memorably started with the line 'All my family want a dog but can't have one because my dad says so'. Nice.

They were relentless – which, true to form, only served to stiffen my resolve. I tried the delaying tactic of getting goldfish, but Norbet and Sparkles died within a week and I fear only increased the kids' desire for pets in general – and a dog in particular. Next, I went to the impressive length of getting a gerbil. This was a disastrous mistake – the sodding thing just sat in its expensive cage, eating leaves.

'It's no fun, Dad,' Alex said.

'Yeah, you can't take it for a walk *like a dog*,' Harry agreed.

'It's boring, Daddy. Why can't we have a dog?' Grace added.

'Promise if we got a dog we'd look after it for you, Daddy,' Eve lied.

The day after this exchange, Kate phoned me at work to tell me a friend's dog had had a litter of puppies and one needed a home. I responded with a ferocious tirade about how much I hated dogs and desperately didn't want one, had never wanted one and never made any secret of the fact. How it pissed me off that it obviously seemed completely fine to everyone to just ignore my heartfelt feelings and go on about it. I ended the call with some choice language expressing the finality of my 'we'll get a dog over my dead body' position.

Kate was more than a little surprised, therefore, when I came home from work that evening, walked into the kitchen and announced, 'Kids, we're getting a dog.'

All four of them jumped up and down, screaming and yelling with delight. They rushed over and gave me the biggest group hug a father has ever received.

Kate rolled her eyes and stared at me with an 'I can't believe what you'll do for attention' look on her face.

'When, Daddy? When are we going to get one?' Grace asked.

'Tonight,' I replied. And that was that.

We didn't have a dog basket, lead, bowl or indeed clue, but there and then we drove to our friends' and picked up the then yet-to-be-named puppy.

Everything I dreaded came true. And worse. The first time I took it out with me was to see Harry play in a rugby game for the Clovelly Eagles at Nagle Park in Maroubra. Up until then, I had refused to take it anywhere. Kate had insisted I grow up, promising me, 'She's such a good dog, Nigel, she'll just sit at your feet and keep you company.'

Which is precisely what she did. At first. Kate had implored me not to keep Mattie on the lead the whole time and, as I looked at her tied up, sitting obediently at my feet, I softened. *What harm could it do*, I reasoned. *She's just sitting there. Keeping her on a lead for no good reason is simply cruel*, I thought as I unclipped her lead and ruffled the fur behind her ears.

Mattie instantly sprang to her feet and ran onto the pitch. A number of parents tutted as she scampered between the legs of the young players who were all crowded at one end of the pitch during a particularly promising scrum move that had threatened to result in a try for Harry's team – until the referee had been forced to blow the whistle because of some idiot's dog.

A couple of the players tried to grab Mattie. She was far too fast for any seven-year-old boy. It was as if she was playing to the crowd as she did one speedy loop of the players, all the while bent low to the ground with only her tail held high, before hurtling off to the middle of the pitch. Upon reaching the centre circle, she stopped, put both of her back legs forward and held still. It dawned on me that I hadn't brought a plastic bag with me as Mattie squeezed out a huge, light-brown soggy turd in the exact spiral shape that ice cream is delivered to your cone from one of those vans.

Marvellous.

Every day, I'd shout at her. Usually, first thing in the morning, when she'd eagerly jump up at me and unwittingly scratch my bare shins, and then again at night, when I came home and in her excitement to see me she'd wee on the hall carpet. Every week, Kate and I would have at least one vicious argument based around her far-from-unreasonable hope that I would actually help with the family pet and my intense irritation at ever being asked to have anything to do with the loathsome beast.

I never referred to her as anything other than 'it' or 'that bloody dog'.

Until a strange thing happened.

I started to like her.

And then, even more bizarrely, love her.

For weeks, despite all my appalling behaviour, she had never once failed to immediately throw herself on her back, front paws floppily bent, eyes adoringly gazing at me, whenever she saw me. To start with, I just ignored her and stepped over her on my way to wherever I was going. However, once, in a relaxed and happy mood, I made the effort to stop, bend down and tickle her tummy like she wanted. The effect was wonderful – she closed her eyes and, I swear, purred. I did it again the next time. And the next.

I found myself disappointed when she wasn't at the door to greet me the next day, as Kate had taken her to a friend's. I started to look forward to taking her for a walk last thing at night. It was a wonderful excuse to have a relaxed chat with Kate. Even hold her hand. I began to enjoy seeing Mattie play with other dogs in the park. I started to *volunteer* to take her with me to places.

One Sunday, Kate and I even had an argument over who was to take her out – as we *both* wanted to. More importantly, I opened my eyes to the amazing effect she was having on the children. Kate had been right – again. They adored Mattie. Were constantly playing with her, stroking and talking to her. Crucially, I could see a more permanent change. Previously, I had been passing my fear of dogs onto my kids – to the extent that they couldn't enjoy other people's pets or even relax in a park when dogs were present (told you I was a wuss). Now, they were developing a genuine and touching affection for every bloody dog, not just our own.

I knew my conversion was complete when a few weeks later, while at the beach, I found myself ditsily running up to a parent, who was looking worried as Mattie yapped at her scared child, and breathlessly uttering the words 'no worries, her bark is worse than her bite, she's never attacked anyone – she's just being friendly'.

There's none so virtuous as a reformed whore, as my dad always used to say.

Kate and I disagree on the lesson from the Mattie experience. She feels it proves that I am 'a hypocritical wanker with a God complex who will do anything for the praise of his children'. While she may have a point, I feel there is a deeper lesson. I am glad I spent so long insisting so vocally that I would never get a dog. The fact that I now have one, and enjoy having one, is a wonderful piece of unarguable personal evidence for me that taking a definitive position on anything is rarely the sensible thing to do. One of my favourite writers is Somerset Maugham. At the end of his long life, he wrote a book called *The Summing Up*, which set out all his life lessons. It's nowhere near as good as his other stuff, but it does contain the wonderful conclusion that 'there is only one thing about which I am certain, and that is there is very little about which one can be certain'. Brilliant.

That, I think, is the point. If I can so radically change my mind about something I was so implacably and vehemently opposed to, how can I be so sure about other stuff? Forget dog ownership – if I can't get it right regarding the merits of having a pet, what possible hope have I got with politics? Or religion? Or macro-economics? Maybe it's not such a bad thing to be able to change your mind. Perhaps it's a sign of strength, not weakness. In fact, maybe it's a good idea to have a life philosophy of positively striving to retain an open mind to the possibility of having your position changed *on everything*. It certainly keeps you on your toes. This is not to say you shouldn't have strong, passionate views – just that you should be alive to the notion that no one has an absolute monopoly on the truth, and that others have every right to hold differing opinions to yours. Perhaps the best we can hope for in this life is to express our views as we see them at the time with the evidence available to us, all the while humbly accepting that those views may change as the evidence does. Admittedly, it is less neat and definitive, but it seems an altogether healthier world view. Indeed, one that would lead to considerably less division and misery if it were adopted at the governmental level. Perish the thought, but maybe the other party *has* got a point. Perhaps the other 'side' *aren't* complete cretins.

I now try to remind myself of this observation whenever Kate is driving me to distraction with her ridiculous point of view that the quickest way to the office in North Sydney is through the Eastern Distributor – rather than my obviously faster, regular route via Ocean Street and the Cahill Expressway . . .

Reach for the Floor

For many of us, there are issues in our lives that just seem so large, we conclude there is nothing worthwhile we can do about them. A friend of Kate's recounts an incident that illustrates this wonderfully. After many years of smoking and little exercise, Ayesha made the radical decision to get fit before she turned forty. To aid her in this process, she consulted a personal trainer. He was pre-eminent in his field and very serious about his craft.

His first session with every new client was to assess what would be a realistic goal. He had a poster stuck on the wall above his desk that plotted seven levels of fitness. Number one was 'Olympic Athlete'. Number seven was 'Dangerously Unfit'. Between them, in descending order, were 'Very Fit',

'Fit', 'Averagely Fit', 'Averagely Unfit' and 'Very Unfit'. The assessment process involved a series of sophisticated and quite demanding tests – running on a treadmill for a set amount of time while hooked up to a monitor and the like.

Having completed all the assessment exercises, Ayesha showered and changed before returning to her trainer's office for the all-important goal-setting discussion.

'Good work this afternoon, Ayesha, really good,' he said. 'You showed admirable application. I feel we could work together well. I only take on clients if they are serious about wanting to change and equally serious about being prepared to put in the required effort. As I explained earlier, the initial goal-setting process is crucial. I believe if you decide to dedicate yourself to this process for an intensive twelve-week period, work hard and do everything I say, we can comfortably guarantee to make you "Averagely Unfit".'

'Averagely *Unfit?*' Ayesha queried.

'Yep,' he replied with inordinate professional pride. 'It's a bit of a stretch, but with hard work and focus I think we can get you there.'

Ayesha was crushed. *What's the point in working your butt off for three months to get 'Averagely Unfit'*, she understandably reasoned. They never did work together.

*

I've come to believe there is an alternative moral to this story beyond 'Ayesha was clearly pretty unfit' or 'her personal trainer was an insensitive twat'. Namely, that if you want to permanently change your life, I believe you should consider *lowering* your standards. Much as I am a fan of raising the bar when appropriate, I feel that sometimes precisely the opposite is required – irrespective of what they say in those self-help books. Insensitive or not, Ayesha's trainer may have had a point.

I passionately believe that lowering, not raising, your sights can be one of the most powerful things you could do if you're after significant and sustainable change in your life. I speak from personal experience, not scientific study. In particular, my running experience.

One of my favourite places to run in Sydney is Centennial Park. My jogs invariably involve a loop of what is known as the Grand Drive. This is the main thoroughfare round the middle of the park, a three and a half kilometre long, tree-lined circular drive in the grand tradition of Victorian parks. A white wooden fence marks it the whole way around, with a dirt horse track and asphalt jogging path alongside. It's like Sydney's version of that running track in New York's Central Park around the Jacqueline

Kennedy Onassis Reservoir – a central feature of the life of both park and city. On a normal day, it is teeming with joggers, runners and walkers.

I tend to run at an unfeasibly slow pace – more waddling than jogging – my main objective being to concentrate on enjoying the experience and my surroundings, as opposed to 'going for the burn'. On these runs, every shape, size, age and dress code is represented – fat people, thin people, grey baggy tracky-dak-wearing men, brightly coloured skin-tight-Lycra-wearing women, men pushing baby joggers, women with iPods, men carrying individual hand weights, old ones, young ones – the whole of the human spectrum seems to be on show. Despite this immense variety, however, they all seem to have one thing in common.

Derek Clayton.

They all appear to have what I call the Derek Clayton Syndrome.

Let me explain.

Derek Clayton is the best marathon runner Australia has ever produced. He was the first athlete to break the two-hour, ten-minute barrier, then again, a few months later, the first to break two hours, nine minutes. The world record he set in Antwerp in 1969 (2:08:33) stood for twelve years. *Twelve* years.

His records aren't why I mention him, though. I mention him because of the announcement he made when he retired. Before I get to that, I should briefly give you a bit of context about his training methods. Derek Clayton was entirely self-trained. And what a training program. At his peak, he was running 200 miles a week – at near on five-minute-mile. It is difficult to fully comprehend how truly impressive that is as a regimen. Comparing it with my own may help: I do *seven miles* a week at eleven-minute-mile pace. To do 200 miles a week involves a depth of commitment that is impossible to overstate. To follow his training regimen would basically mean your life involved nothing other than eating, sleeping and running.

Now, I want you to bear in mind the above time commitment when you read the statement below that Clayton made upon announcing his retirement:

'I can honestly admit now that I never enjoyed a single minute of my running.'

What an idiot.

What an incredible, mind-numbingly stupid waste of time.

No, that's not fair. I don't know what demons drove Clayton.

But I *do* know that in a normal case, to do something for so long, so often, so joylessly is not heroic – it is moronic. And that's what I mean by the Derek Clayton Syndrome – joylessly and grimly pursuing a goal while all the time hating the journey.

Life is too short. It really is.

I'm not suggesting you have to jog around the Grand Drive grinning like an idiot and saying hello to the trees like I do. I am, however, suggesting that it is a worthwhile idea to attempt to enjoy the moment at the same time that you pursue whatever personal goal it is you have set. The vast majority of people I pass (or, more accurately, who pass *me*) on the Grand Drive look as if they are hating every minute of it. I just refuse to believe that if they enjoyed it more (slowed down, went with a friend, shortened the route, skipped, whatever), their figure or fitness would suffer. In fact, I'm convinced both would benefit. You tend to stick at what you enjoy, after all.

Having been unfair to Clayton (who I don't know from Adam), I should mention here that after he retired he gave up running completely for a while. Then he returned to the sport – with a new attitude and a new training regimen. He happily settled into a routine of five-mile runs. Nothing to base a world record on, but in my humble opinion as valuable a life lesson as you're ever likely to get from sport.

On reflection, perhaps I should call it the Nigel Marsh Syndrome instead because, truth be told, I started out trying to be a bit of a Derek Clayton myself. I got the running bug as a young man living and working in London. I'd never been into athletics as a kid; never run seriously at all, in fact. But at the ripe old age of twenty-eight, I suddenly decided that jogging was the method of exercise I was going to take up. As I said earlier, I like a goal, so I set myself the target of running the London marathon that very same year. I sent off my application and set about training in earnest. Ten weeks later, I developed a chronic case of shin splints due to overtraining and had to stop running altogether until well after the event.

Undeterred, I bought a stopwatch and ran three times around my local park. My new target was to run the same course three times a week – each time at a faster pace until I could do it at five minutes a mile. The only record I broke was that this time it was only six weeks before I was injured. I continued in this self-defeating vein for more than a year until a conversation with a colleague changed my strategy – and my life.

'Nigel, how long have you been trying and failing to set up a regular running routine?' he asked.

'Since a few months before last year's marathon – 'bout seventeen months,' I replied.

'And in that time, how many races have you done?'

'None – always injured myself training for them.'

'Okay. I've got an idea for you,' he said. 'If you're open to suggestion, that is.'

I assured him I was only too open – anything had to be better than what I'd been doing.

'I want you to change your mindset. Don't train for an event – don't even time yourself. Concentrate instead on enjoying each run,' he advised. 'Notice the weather and the nature around you. Look at other runners grimly pounding around the park and remind yourself to smile. Do eight weeks of never running for longer than twenty minutes at a time and never doing two days in a row. Every time you feel tired, stop and walk. Make an effort to think of pleasant things. And never – repeat never – succumb to the "no pain, no gain" mind chatter.'

'So basically you want me to change my goal of "run

the London marathon in under four hours" to "do twenty-eight short, slow runs within two months"?' I asked.

'Yep.'

'Doesn't sound hard enough,' I said.

'Not sure the "hard" goals are working for you, mate,' he replied.

To cut a long story short, I managed to reach my new target of twenty-eight gentle jogs in two months. That initial goal was eclipsed, however, by the lifelong benefit of my new attitude. I actually enjoyed each and every run. I started to look forward to them, as opposed to dreading them. I didn't get injured. I lost some weight. I began to appreciate things on my runs that I hadn't even noticed before, due to my grim determination to push myself as hard as possible.

I decided to extend the initial goal to include another two months of running without injury – same rules. I happily met that target as well. The end result of my experiment with a lower aspiration is that I have now enjoyed more than ten years of injury-free running. *By lowering my standards, I dramatically increased my achievement.*

Whenever I tell this story, people object that lowering your standards and setting 'small' goals is all well and good, but surely it must inevitably mean never achieving anything BIG?

I believe the reverse is the case. Repeated, consistent small victories *turn into* big victories. Lowering your standards doesn't mean giving up on grand inspiring dreams. It means giving yourself more chance of actually reaching them.

A few years back, I couldn't swim. I was immersed in my mid-life crisis and set myself the ridiculous goal of competing in the Bondi to Bronte rough-water ocean race. Bearing in mind the lesson from my running experience, I set a series of pathetically minute targets – as insignificant as 'swim one length of a thirty-metre pool' and 'get in a pool three times this week'.

Each time I reached a milestone (however small), I congratulated myself and increased it by a fraction for the following week. This is not advice for serious athletes – in fact, it's not advice for anyone. It's just what worked for me. I completed the race in December 2005. I came second last.

It didn't feel like second last, though – it felt utterly wonderful.

As I came out of the surf and crossed the finishing line, Kate and all four of our kids rushed up to congratulate me.

As they were doing so, a photographer interrupted us.

'Excuse me – are you Nigel Marsh?'

'Yep,' I confirmed.

'*The* Nigel Marsh?'

'Er, dunno – *a* Nigel Marsh.'

'Are you the bloke who wrote *Fat, Forty and Fired*?'

'Yeah.'

'So you've finally done it! Congratulations. I'm from the *Daily Telegraph* and I need a few pictures for tomorrow's paper, if you don't mind.'

'Daddy, you're famous!' Eve gasped in wide-eyed amazement.

'Oh, not really, sweetheart,' I replied modestly, at the same time thinking, *Dead right I am!*

He then got me to pose by the finishing line in a variety of positions, with and without the family.

After the impromptu photo shoot, I walked up to the surf club at the back of the beach to be met by two friends bent double with laughter. Turns out the photographer was indeed from the *Daily Telegraph*. He just wasn't there for *me*. He'd been sent to get pictures of the winners. As a joke, my friends had talked him into waiting for the hour or so it took me to finish and pretend to be interested in taking my picture. Hook, line and sinker, as they say.

To the photographer's credit, he sent me a copy of one of the photos which, to this day, I've got framed above my desk. As both a reminder of how small goals can lead to big achievements and also of how vanity, not just pride, can lead to a fall.

Shamefully, I still haven't told Eve the truth, however.

Because You're Worth it

Throwing in my job has meant we've had to implement a few radical changes to our lifestyle. The simple economics of the situation demanded that immediate and permanent savings be made. Foreign holidays were cancelled, the nanny bade farewell and thoughts of the new second car I'd recently test-driven banished. Granted, nothing to complain about, but still an adjustment for a family of six used to an existence that didn't involve counting every cent on a daily basis.

At the same time that these big changes were being put in place, I also began to experiment with a whole raft of smaller ones. I've long since thought that a stress-filled professional life can lead to otherwise sensible people unwittingly and habitually spending more money than they need. If you can afford to pay $4 for your morning coffee and you're in a rush to get to work, it can quickly become part of your routine to piss thousands of dollars a year down the dunny on low-quality, overpriced long blacks. Well, it did for me, anyway. Looking back and thinking about it for a few moments, it soon becomes blindingly obvious that you could just as easily have made your own and saved a motza. But it's easy to be wise after the event, and of course in my CEO days I never did bring in a packed lunch or think twice about popping across the street from the office for an expensive take-away coffee. Now that I was once again attempting to survive outside the corporate battery coop, I decided to do an audit of the things I spent money on and, as far as possible, cut out needless purchases – however ingrained they may have become.

After a short period of contemplation, I was able to draw up a long list of minor changes I wanted to try to implement. Both to save money and, as the Quakers say, to attempt to live a simpler life.

Ridiculous as it may sound, the item at the top of this list was 'hair'. I wouldn't even have thought hair would *make* the list, as I've always been pretty spartan about my mop-care regimen. I've never had it permed or dyed or whatever and resolutely refuse to use gel or a hairdryer. Strictly low-maintenance is the strategy. But despite this, I couldn't rid myself of the nagging suspicion that I was still acting gratuitously simply out of a subliminal desire to conform to society's expectations of what was normal.

The first change was to stop going to the hairdresser I'd used as a CEO. I have to say, he is a top bloke and gives a damn fine haircut. But he is, shall we say, at the successful businessman end of the hairdressing spectrum, not the struggling author end. Much as I love the head massages, coffees and respectful chat, it's pushing it slightly to claim this fits within any credible definition of a 'simple life'.

I therefore resolved to find a cheaper, more basic way of keeping my hair short. I debated having Kate cut it but, as she pointed out, as I was regularly giving leadership speeches to business audiences, we decided the 'my wife has just been hacking at my head with the kitchen scissors' look was probably not a good one.

Making the decision to go basic and actually doing it were two different things entirely. Finding the type of place I was after was no small feat. I didn't know whether it was the area I lived in or simply hairdressing salons generally, but they all seemed to have gone upmarket. And had bloody stupid names. At least my previous one was called George. Because he was called George. This lot seemed to be addicted to the type of crap puns I thought only Thai restaurants went in for. I'd never noticed it before, but the monikers were truly awful – Hairforce, HeadHunters, Hair I Go, Beauticious, HairFidelity. Just as I was running out of hope and driving home, I came across exactly what I was looking for barely a few blocks from our house. I'd never noticed it before, which I suppose is a pretty powerful example of selective perception. Why would I have noticed? It wasn't the sort of place a CEO would normally be seen dead in. It had one of those red and white swirly poles outside and the name above the front window was written in simple capitals, straightforwardly proclaiming 'BARBER'. Perfect.

It had been a while since my last haircut and, as I could see a park a few metres down the street, I pulled in and decided to visit there and then. A bell jangled as I opened the door, alerting the large Eastern European lady who was cutting an elderly gent's hair in the sole barber's chair to my presence. 'Take seat,' she said, motioning with her scissors to the plastic chair in front of me.

She turned back to her work while I sat and surveyed the surroundings. 'No frills' would just about catch it. Worn, fading lino on the floor. Hideous black and white photos of strangely coiffed blokes on the walls. No air-conditioning. Transistor radio tuned to a non-English-speaking station on the partition between the 'barber' bit of the room and the 'family living room' bit of the room. It powerfully reminded me of the places I used to get my hair cut as a kid. Basic but clean.

I didn't have to wait long – she was soon finished with her first client. His hair looked all right to me, and I noticed approvingly that when he stood up to pay, he reached in his pocket and pulled out not an Amex or a fifty-dollar note but a ten. And he got change.

As I took his place in the barber's chair, I started my 'briefing'. I've always been nervous in hairdressers, never knowing precisely what to say beyond, 'I'd like to look like David Beckham, please.'

'Hi, nothing fancy, thanks,' I started. 'If you could take an inch off the sides and thin out the top a bit, that would be great. Sideburns shaved off as well, if that's all right. And I part it to the left, so if you could –'

'Yes, yes. A *haircut*,' she witheringly interrupted.

Barely ten minutes later, she was finished and I, too, was handing over a ten-dollar note. The change didn't include a fiver, but it was enough to enable me to piss yet more family funds up the wall on an expensive latte in the coffee shop next door.

No surprise to report that in the following days, no one, simply no one, felt moved to point out, 'Nige, your hair looks shocking – you haven't gone and spent $100 less on it than usual, have you?'

I like to think this is not because they were being polite, but simply because it looked exactly the same as if I *had* spent $100 on it. Whatever – I'm now a regular and, lack of pun notwithstanding, the 'Barber' suits me fine.

The success of my experiment not only saved me a few bucks, it also spurred me on in my quest to 'economise and simplify'. No sooner had I discovered that the world didn't stop spinning if I no longer had $100 haircuts than I started to wonder if it was really necessary for me to wash my hair with the ridiculously expensive shampoo we had fallen into the trap of buying. Don't get me wrong

– we didn't set out to waste money on pricey shampoo. We had just arrived at the end of that seemingly irresistible process where every year you try the latest product or new 'innovation' and suddenly, hey presto, after fifteen years of marriage you've got a fourteen-dollar bottle of shampoo in your shower. *And it seems normal.*

I read the label on the current bottle in our bathroom and was surprised to learn it wasn't even called shampoo – it was instead 'an essential part of a daily haircare regimen'. Oh, and it was also 'specifically designed' for my 'particular hair-type needs'. Whatever that meant. I had become yet another muppet worn down by the never-ending drip, drip, drip of marketing exhortations imploring me to ever greater indulgence while washing my hair. Apparently, accordingly to those ridiculous TV ads, I was worth it.

I spent a moment debating what my real haircare needs were and how best to serve them. After long and intensive thought, I decided that 'keep my hair clean' seemed to pretty much cover it. I then got to questioning if I really needed to wash and condition my hair three times a week with expensive, ludicrously packaged products to achieve this modest aim. Could it be possible that twice a week would do? I know people who wash their hair *every* day and it never seems any cleaner than mine. Perhaps I could cut down to once a week? When I was a child, we used to wash our hair once a fortnight with revolting, watery, homebrand gunk and that had always worked fine. Heck, I wondered what would happen if I reverted to my childhood routine? Apart, of course, from saving buckets of cash.

Ten minutes of this idle musing and I was suddenly hit by a gorgeously radical notion. What if I stopped washing my hair altogether? I don't know why but at that moment it just seemed the obvious thing to do.

So I did.

Now, I need to point out I've no desire to walk around with greasy or smelly hair. I am as vain (or vainer, according to Kate) as the next man. I don't want to make a statement with my hair. I don't want to have dreadlocks, either. I just wanted to discover if it was possible to opt out of the bullshit and make a minor personal stand against mindless commercialism and crass environmental irresponsibility. And still have clean hair.

I was embarrassed about my scheme at first, so I didn't mention it to anyone. I just stopped washing my hair.

I still had showers and baths, but instead of reaching for the shampoo bottle I simply rubbed my head under the water, unadulterated with any soap or shampoo. Every day, I worried that Kate would crinkle her nose in disgust or someone would point out that my hair needed a wash, but days – then weeks – passed and nothing happened. I had to attend a variety of formal functions during this time, so it's not as if I was getting away with it because I was living the life of a crusty beach bum. It really didn't seem to matter. Had I been pouring hundreds of dollars of cash (and pollution) down the drain each year for no good reason? Just as it seemed so, my younger son, Harry, threatened to burst my bubble.

'Daddy?' he said as I was coming down the stairs one evening.

'Yes, mate,' I replied.

'Your hair looks different,' he remarked, a questioning tone in his voice.

'Really, sweetheart?' I responded, bracing myself for the worst. 'How do you mean?'

Harry looked at my head carefully for a minute. 'It's going grey,' he observed. 'Like an old man,' he unnecessarily added.

'Anything else?'

'Nah. Apart from all the grey, it looks the same. Luv ya,' he said before bouncing off.

I know I should have been crushed, but I was actually elated. And haven't looked back since. It's been more than a year now since I washed my hair, and I swear you wouldn't be able to tell me apart from a three-times-a-week man, however hard you looked, felt or smelt.

I'm not advocating this approach for anyone else. (Although having said that, a few months after I stopped washing my hair, a Sydney radio show got 500 listeners – male and female – to stop washing their hair for six weeks. At the end of the experiment, eighty-seven per cent of them said they would never use shampoo again . . .) Frankly, it's none of my business what you decide to do with your hair – and let's face it, there are far more important things to worry about than shampoo.

I am saying, however, that it can be a worthwhile process to look at how you can simplify your life.

Before I came to Australia, I wore a tie to the office every single working day of my life. It took me a while to adjust, but after a year of living in Sydney I stopped wearing them. Haven't worn one to the office in more than four years. And what has been the downside? None. Just saved a bunch of money, felt more comfortable and marginally spared the Earth's resources into the bargain. I'm convinced that if we really examine it, there are always a number of things we can usefully eradicate from our lives. And not just trivial things like shampoo or ties but more significant things, such as unhealthy negative relationships or the search for external affirmations.

The whole shampoo thing has led me to another related observation. All too often we decide on an objective (be it clean hair, getting fit, happiness or providing for our family financially) and then become fixated and rigid on one particular strategy to reach that objective. A hundred years ago, well before any of our currently famous self-help gurus were born, Nietzsche wrote, 'Many are stubborn in the pursuit of the path they have chosen, few in pursuit of the goal.' It's a remark that I feel is every bit as relevant today. All too often and too readily we seem to lose sight of our initial goal, and instead rigorously and determinedly cling to *the ways* we've decided to reach this goal, however ineffective they prove to be. To my mind, a bit more flexibility around your strategies in life isn't a sign of weakness or lack of focus – it's just plain good sense. If what you're doing isn't working, my observation is that to blindly continue to do it makes you uncomfortably like one of those flies that desperately keep buzzing into the glass door in an attempt to get outside while all the time, just to the side, there is an open window. A far worse – tragic, even – response to an ineffectual strategy is *to give up on your goal*. This mistake keeps millions of us from fulfilling our true potential.

Just maybe we should all be a bit more comfortable with trying different paths to where we want to go.

Just the One

Whatever certain self-help books may imply, successfully implementing meaningful permanent changes in your life is always a challenge. I'm a great believer in the 'nothing worthwhile is easy' school of thought. Trouble is, when you're trying to change you don't have to just deal with your own demons – you frequently have to deal with other people's as well.

Five years ago I gave up alcohol. Whenever pressed to talk about this decision in awkward circumstances I quote Scottish comedian Billy Connolly, who once said, 'Every man has a bucket of booze to drink in his lifetime – I just happened to finish mine early.' It's a story I use to avoid long explanations.

Long or short explanation, there's no hiding the fact that it wasn't an easy thing to do. It took determination and constant vigilance. It still does. Especially in social situations.

Now, over the past five years of sobriety I have gone back to the UK once a year to visit my family. These trips always involve a dinner at my Uncle David's house in Newcastle.

David knows I've given up the booze. Imagine my surprise therefore when, having recently given up drinking, we arrived at his front door and the very first words out of his mouth were: 'Nigel! Hi! Can I get you a nice cold beer?'

I politely declined and let it pass.

Thing is, he did the same the next year. And the next.

This year, before we got on the plane for our annual trip I said to Kate, 'I hope Uncle David doesn't offer me a nice cold beer this time.'

'Don't worry,' Kate said. 'I'm sure he won't.'

Forty-eight hours later I was greeted by David at his front door.

'Nigel! Hi! Can I get you a nice cold beer?'

'No thanks, David,' I replied.

A couple of hours later as we were sitting down for dinner he turned to me and said, 'Nigel, can I fix you a glass of wine?'

'No thanks, David,' I said quietly. 'I've given up drink.'

'Yes, I know. But I wondered if you'd like just the one glass to go with the meal?'

'David!' his wife, Margaret, interrupted angrily. 'He's given up alcohol. He hasn't had a drink in four years!'

'I know,' David replied. 'I just thought he may have grown up a bit since we last saw him.'

To be fair to David (who I love dearly, by the way) he called up and apologised later. He explained that he was trying to be a good host and my refusal of the offer of a drink and his wife's remarks made him feel awkward and put on the spot. So he simply said the first thing that entered his head.

It's not the first time I've been put in a compromising situation because of my abstinence. And I'm sure it won't be the last; because giving up drink is such a difficult decision for many people to understand. If you don't get the whole addiction thing it can be thought of as merely a fleeting and irritating affectation. Especially if you aren't the classic 'down and out' drunk. Many people have a fixed mental image of an alcoholic – a bottle-of-whisky-a-day-drinking, car-crashing, gutter-lying destitute bed wetter. If you have done none of those things and indeed you're successfully holding down a job then by definition you can't have a 'real' drink problem. But anyone who has watched a loved one struggling with this issue knows that, of course this is total nonsense. There are countless people out there who, on the surface, are coping, but whose emotional and family lives are in turmoil because of their dependence on alcohol. And that's not to mention the devastating long-term health consequences.

I've recently become friendly with a doctor who is preeminent in the field of substance abuse. She has a phrase to describe functioning alcoholics – rather than down and outs she calls them 'up and outs'. She maintains they are a surprisingly large group, and that being one involves a number of unique problems. Problems that, as a society, we are only starting to come to grips with. I wouldn't claim to fully comprehend all the nuances of her medical and social theories but I do know from personal experience that many people do find it difficult to understand why I can't have just the one. Fact is for me, and many others, there is no such thing as 'just the one'. Moreover, just the one is *precisely* the thing to avoid at all costs. To a non-alcoholic it is the smallest most insignificant thing to suggest, but to an alcoholic it is the most dangerous threat there is. Indeed 'never pick up the first drink' is one of the central lessons you hear repeated again and again at AA. With such a gargantuan difference in perspective on this 'just the one' point it is no wonder social misunderstandings frequently occur.

Whatever the complexities of this issue in general, the 'Newcastle incident' in particular does serve as a useful reminder to me that if you want to change something about your life, you have to want to do it for *yourself*, and be prepared to do it *by yourself*, first and foremost. Irrespective of whether you're trying to kick the smokes, lose weight or give up the grog, if you are doing it for *external* validation – or if you've based your plans for change on the assumption that everyone around you will understand – you're in for a fall.

Genius

Despite the evidence of my no-shampoo policy, Kate thinks I'm vain. I don't agree with her. I haven't got that much to be vain about. And anyway, life always seems to deal me an appropriate blow just when it could look like she might be about to get the ammunition to back up her belief.

If I was vain (which I'm not), my vanity would have been nicely pricked when I was invited to a thing called the NISAD ball.

NISAD (the Neuroscience Institute of Schizophrenia and Allied Disorders) is a worthy charity – worthy in the good sense – in support of schizophrenia research. Every year, it holds a fundraising ball. This takes place in Sydney's Town Hall and is generally regarded as a big deal – all red carpet, TV cameras, B-list celebs and bling. In 2006, the ball was entitled 'Spark of Genius', the idea being that thirty or so geniuses would each host a table. The ten seats on each table would then be sold at a steep price to paying punters. The list of 'geniuses' was rather impressive – David Helfgott, Reg Mombassa, Andrew Denton, Bill Granger . . . and *me*. When I got the invitation, I genuinely thought there had been a mistake. When I found out there hadn't, and that they really did want me, I was enormously embarrassed – but secretly thrilled.

A month or so before the big day, we received a letter from the organising committee asking the geniuses if they needed to be put up for the night at the Hotel InterContinental. Obviously, this offer was intended for those who'd have to travel from interstate or overseas, not someone like me, who lived barely six kilometres away. An offer is an offer, however, and with four young kids I'm always on the lookout for anything that could just possibly create the right environment for the potential of actually having sex with my wife, so I wrote back saying that yes, I would like to be put up for the night.

The night itself started with a cocktail party in the InterContinental's thirty-third-floor bar overlooking the Sydney Harbour Bridge and Opera House, a wonderful setting in which the geniuses could get to know each other before being driven to the Town Hall to mix with ordinary mortals.

When I arrived, the party had split into discrete little groups of five or six people doing that cocktail party chit-chat thing. I joined the nearest group and made polite conversation.

After a few minutes, the group fell silent. 'So who *are* you?' the person opposite me asked.

'Nigel Marsh,' I replied.

'And why are you here?'

'I think it's because I've written a book,' I said.

'Really? And what's it called?'

'*Fat, Forty and Fired.*'

The moment I uttered that title, a woman behind me burst into our group excitedly.

'*Fat, Forty and Fired*? *Fat, Forty and Fired*?' she said. 'My best friend gave me that book yesterday! She said it was fantastic, funny and inspiring . . . but that the bloke in it was obviously a right fucker.'

My new genius friends looked at me expectantly.

'Er . . . *I* wrote it,' I hesitantly admitted.

'Yes, yes, but you're not the bloke *in* it,' she insisted.

'Well, I am, actually,' I rather feebly replied.

Clearly, not really a genius at all. I didn't get laid, either.

Much as we may not enjoy it at the time, I feel it is almost always a good thing to be brought down to earth. Humility is such an underrated quality in today's success-obsessed society. Time and again I've seen people spoilt by even a modicum of success. They start to feel they are not only different to 'ordinary' people but that they are somehow better than them as well. A sad consequence of this feeling of superiority in many cases is that they lose their capacity to empathise with people of modest means and circumstances. It is as if they've joined an exclusive club of well-off achievers and a condition of membership is that henceforth their circle of concern has to be limited solely to other club members. In short, they become less human.

It is not just our increasingly vacuous media-driven society that is to blame for this tendency towards conceited self-importance. However humble we may like to believe we are, it's a hardwired human failing to have a tendency to believe your own bullshit given half an ounce of encouragement. I was reminded of this fact a couple of years ago when I enjoyed a little bit of media attention after my first book was published in Australia.

My fifteen minutes of fame was strictly minor-league stuff – a couple of TV interviews and magazine stories – but still enough for the corrosive siren call of celebrity to go to work on my pitiable ego. The writer John Updike was of the opinion that 'celebrity is a mask that eats into the face of those who wear it' and, on the evidence of this particular incident, I'm inclined to agree.

Returning from a business trip to Melbourne late one night, I climbed, exhausted, into a cab at the airport.

'Macpherson Street, please,' I said.

The cabbie looked at me quizzically. 'Don't tell me,' he replied. 'It'll come to me . . .'

He put his head down in thought for a moment, then looked up at me questioningly again and said, 'It's right on the tip of my tongue, but I can't place it . . . I'm sorry, would you mind telling me . . .'

'Of course. It's Nigel Marsh. You're probably remembering the Mel and Kochie interview on *Sunrise* . . . that's the one most people have seen,' I said.

'Not tell me your name, you dickhead,' he replied. 'I mean, tell me where Macpherson Street is.'

Mask or no mask, fifteen minutes is clearly long enough for me.

Steve Waugh

I seem to have a mysterious genetic ability to attract events and circumstances that regularly cut me down to size. A recent speaking engagement on Hayman Island was a perfect example. It was for one of the four big banks. A prestigious gig. And what's more, I was to be the keynote speaker. The location wasn't half bad, either. Hayman Island, in the Whitsundays, is basically a rich man's playground on the coral reef. It was the sort of destination Kate and I could no longer afford. To be visiting all-expenses-paid topped things off nicely. Well, for me, anyway, as Kate had to stay at home to look after the kids. I almost felt guilty.

All thoughts of others soon evaporated, however, when the plane touched down on Hamilton Island and I was escorted to the boat that was to take me the fifty minutes across the clear blue sea to the smaller and more remote Hayman. *Screw climbing the corporate ladder in an office,* I thought. *I may be poorer, but this is living.* I settled back into the plush seat on the open-air top deck and mused on my good fortune.

I felt so very lucky to have stumbled into a second career as a public speaker. It plays to my fondness for presenting to a crowd (or my 'rampant narcissism', as Kate puts it) but there are many other things I love about it. For a start, the flexibility of the work is perfect for the new life I am attempting to pursue. I have a rule: do no more than one gig a week. However far afield I have to travel, this gives me ample opportunity to write and to spend time with the family. Time which in my previous life would have been spent away from them in an office.

Perhaps above all I cherish the opportunity public speaking gives me to chat to individual audience members either side of the official engagement. I always accept invites to functions before or after my speeches. I find talking with so many new and varied people genuinely fascinating – people I would never have had the chance to meet if it wasn't for the gig. I particularly enjoy the feedback people give me, however robust. I'm yet to come away from an event without having learnt something unexpected and valuable. And, of course, the locations have a tendency to be wonderful as large companies usually try to take their employees somewhere impressive for their conferences.

There was only one other person on the boat with me. I'd paid him no attention, as I'd been too busy counting my blessings, but now I looked at him, he seemed vaguely familiar. Was he a parent at the school? Or someone from the surf club? I couldn't quite place him. As he had a hat and glasses on, it wasn't easy to identify him, so I gave up and gazed back at the view. The instant I gave up trying to place him, it came to me in a flash – fuck me sideways, it was none other than Steve Waugh!

Alex and Harry would go mental when I told them. The 2006–07 Ashes campaign had just started, so the timing couldn't have been better for such a chance meeting. I tried to resist the temptation to be so naff as to approach him and start a conversation. The longer I resisted, however, the more I envisaged the disappointment in my sons' faces when I told them I'd sat next to

Steve Waugh for fifty minutes and not even said hello or got an autograph.

Finally, I gave in, clenched my buttocks and approached the great man. I suppose I shouldn't be surprised, but he was charm personified. Far from making me feel like a dill or a sappy sports fan, he was welcoming and disarmingly humble. He was keen to tell me all about the Steve Waugh Foundation and genuinely excited about the good that he could see it doing for those less fortunate than him.

After fifteen minutes of pleasant conversation, it was possible to kid myself that Steve Waugh was actually my mate and it was natural for us to be on a boat together headed for a posh holiday location.

'So Steve,' I ventured. 'You're off for a bit of rest and relaxation, then? I can well imagine you wanting to get away from it, what with all the work I'm sure you have on during the Ashes series and everything.'

'I wish,' he replied. 'It's not a holiday. I'm doing a spot of work. Can only stay for one night.'

'Oh, really? What type of work is that, then?' I asked, enjoying our boat trip bonding.

'I'm the keynote speaker at a banking conference on the island,' he said.

'No, that can't be right. *I'm* the keynote speaker at the –' My voice trailed off as the penny dropped.

Oh lordy, I thought, *this is a slightly 'sub-optimal context', as they say in the trade.* 'Pommy Non-Entity Follows Australian Icon' was not exactly the set-up I had in mind when I took the engagement. To make matters worse, England had just been given 500-odd runs to chase in the first test in Brisbane, having been humiliatingly whittled out for only 157 runs in their first innings. Humiliation was a word I felt certain I would soon become better acquainted with.

Looking back, the booking had been at short notice. Presumably, no one else was stupid enough to accept a gig following such an out-and-out legend. As I stepped off the boat at Hayman, all thoughts of the gorgeous location and my good fortune had vanished as I contemplated that perhaps a traditional office career wasn't so bad after all.

When I returned to Sydney later that week, I told Kate the story. Putting it down as a 'valuable learning experience', I then stupidly tempted fate.

'Well, after that, nothing can be as embarrassing,' I said.

It only took two weeks for me to be proved wrong.

This time, the gig was in nowhere as glamorous a location as Hayman, but in a standard business hotel in Sydney's Rushcutters Bay, a few ks away from where we live. Not only was there no luxury travel involved, there were no famous people involved, either. Quite the contrary. It was just me, and this time I *was* the keynote speaker.

Even though I say it myself, I thought I stormed the gig. I was on top of my game and full of searing business insights. But something just didn't seem right. People kept giving me funny looks. I stayed for lunch and a chat with the audience after my talk, and although people were verbally very complimentary, the funny looks continued. I couldn't work it out. Maybe I'd lost my humility and become complacent? It can happen to any performer who has to deal with repetition. You get so used to your material that you do an event on autopilot. You neglect to respect – and love – your audience. You forget that you are being paid to entertain *them*, not the other way around. When this happens it always shows. I thought of one of the popstars I'd seen in Sydney recently who had fairly taken my breath away with his lack of commitment to the audience. He had attempted to justify his woeful performance in a post-concert interview with the excuse that it was the end of a long world tour and he was jaded. Poor love. I remember thinking at the time: only paid a couple of million dollars a year and having to put up with all that first-class travel. Heartbreaking.

Was I guilty of the same crime? I didn't feel I'd coasted that day. Every time I speak I try to connect with and 'convert' each and every member of the audience. Of course I never have anything close to 100 per cent success but at least the intention always keeps me alert, present and authentic. Or so I thought.

I didn't think it was lack of commitment therefore that had caused the funny looks, nor the content of my speech, so I was mystified. And worried. This was how I now earnt a living. I couldn't afford to go 'off'. The bookings would dry up and we'd be up shit creek without a financial paddle.

When I got home, I shared my puzzlement with Kate. 'I thought I was good this afternoon, but something about their response wasn't quite right.'

'Do you think *that* might have had anything to do with it?' she asked, pointing at my chest.

I looked down and saw a multicoloured sticker attached to the front of my suit jacket. The sticker was in the shape of a starburst and had written on it, in enormous capitals, the mildly moronic message 'MY NAME IS NIGEL!!' The glitter pen that had been used to write the words topped off the 'manic children's TV presenter' feel nicely.

Actually, it was the remnants of my morning in Bondi, where I'd taken part in my twin daughters' school Marine Exploring Trip. Basically, this had involved helping the teachers out by taking a group of kids to look at rockpools at the north end of the beach. I couldn't stay the whole time as I had to rush off halfway through to do the gig. In my haste, I'd forgotten the sticker the teacher had kindly stuck on my jacket.

That morning, I'd intended to dress as a serious business commentator. Instead, I'd unwittingly done the whole speech dressed as some sort of deranged Wiggle.

When I called the conference organisers to inquire why no one had felt the need to tell me about the sticker, they quite reasonably responded that as I had turned up like that, they'd assumed it was part of my persona. 'A rather sweet but strange attempt to appear approachable' was the phrase the woman used – a phrase that has since stuck in my mind.

On balance, I think I'd rather follow Steve Waugh.

Earthworm

In the face of events like these, vanity is not my problem (whatever Kate may think). Self-esteem is. Not too much of it. Rather, not enough of it. There's a lovely bloke called Peter who lives near me in Bronte. Apart from being a dear friend, he's also my personal coach. I started to use him when I was CEO of Leo Burnett and found it so worthwhile, I kept on seeing him in his official capacity long after the original professional need had gone.

In preparation for one session, Peter asked me to write a list of things I was proud of. All week, I agonised about what I could include in my list. Good father? Author? CEO? Done the City to Surf? Given up drink? Each day, I would anxiously add a few more things.

When we met for our next session, Peter asked me to show him my list. He read it with a thoughtful expression on his face, then asked, 'What do you think when you look at this?'

Oh God, I knew it was pathetically inadequate, I thought. 'Well, obviously that it's not good enough,' I replied.

Silence.

'What do you think?' I asked him.

'Honestly?' Peter said.

'Honestly.'

'That you're showing off,' he said.

And he meant it.

We were both looking at the same list – yet we had utterly different, genuinely felt, responses to it.

All my life, I've been struggling to feed the self-esteem monster. For years now, I have gone through a never-ending process of creating a target and convincing myself that if only I could reach it then, and only then, I would know I was 'all right'. Trouble is, whenever I reached a target, it immediately became irrelevant and I set another one. *If only I could get promoted to MD, I'll know I'm all right.* I'd get promoted to MD and think, *if only I could get promoted to CEO, I'll know I'm all right.* I'd get promoted to CEO and think, *if only I could get the company to double its profits, then I'll know I'm all right.*

My desire to achieve tangible goals and success is not to prove to others that I'm better than them. It is to prove to myself that I'm not a worthless earthworm. This is not false modesty. It's just the exhausting and debilitating truth. I think it stems from being sent away to boarding school at a very early age and therefore feeling the need to do things to gain my parents' attention and affirmation but, quite frankly, I don't care where it comes from – all I know is it has messed me up and led me down the wrong path for far too many years.

I've come to realise that no external achievement is ever going to fill the void within me and finally make me feel I'm all right and worthy. I could win gold at the Olympics and discover the cure for cancer all in the same week and I'd still feel like an idiot *because I didn't discover it early enough and anyway the competitors at this year's Olympics weren't very good so it doesn't really count, does it?* I'm very, very good at negating anything I achieve.

Then again, even if I ever did achieve something that was inarguably impressive, that wouldn't work, either. My friend Todd talks of what he calls Post-traumatic *Success* Syndrome. This is the phrase he uses to sum up how you feel if you ever do get to summit a personal mountain that you've been working towards – one you feel will somehow finally make everything all right.

He should know – he successfully climbed Everest solo, and hearing him talk of his experience after the climb is almost more interesting than the story of the climb itself. He was still the same old Todd when he got back down. Whatever shit you have got to sort out, you have still got to sort it out. As the Olympic athlete Jesse Owens once remarked, 'The only victory that counts is the one over yourself.'

No external victory is ever going to satiate the self-esteem monster – it's a hungry fucker. You don't need to feed it, you need to kill it. And that's a job that needs to be resolved in your heart and mind – not on the sports field, in the boardroom or wherever.

It's taken me a long time to learn that if I want peace and serenity, I have to work on the inside, not the outside. It's about changing my perspective and attitude – not about achieving more.

In this regard, I feel I could (and indeed do) learn a lot from my children. Recently, the Commonwealth Games were held in Melbourne. I had no interest in most of the events but desperately wanted to take my two young sons to the Rugby 7s. I try to take them to as many games as possible. It's a very special and precious ritual in my life. I am paranoid, however, about spoiling my kids. I didn't want my sons thinking it was normal to fly around the country on a weekend and stay in a swanky hotel. So, after booking the cheapest flights available, I went on the net and booked the crappiest central Melbourne hotel I could find.

Sure enough, on arrival, I could see that the hotel was indeed a right dive. *Perfect for my 'build the kids' character' purposes*, I thought as I checked in.

No sooner had I picked up the room key from the front desk, however, than Alex called out to me. 'Dad, Dad,' he said, 'come over here and look at this!' He was wide-eyed with amazement as he pointed to a framed certificate on the wall.

'What is it, sweetheart?' I asked.

'It says here, Dad, that this place won the "best two-star hotel in Melbourne in 1996" award!' he exclaimed.

I need a bit of that – being two-star and proud of it, as opposed to always hankering after some unattainable six-star achievement that wouldn't bring me peace anyway.

Chris Whitaker

I hope I never meet Chris Whitaker.

It's not that I don't like the man. He is in fact a hero of mine. I'm afraid that if I actually met him the reality couldn't possibly live up to my fantasy.

Chris Whitaker is a rugby player. He was selected to represent his country – Australia – over eighty times. No mean feat, given the intense competition to be a Wallaby. This, however, isn't the reason he is my hero. Quite the opposite. It's all the other stuff about him that makes me worship him from afar. You see, he may have been selected eighty-odd times in the course of a ten-year career, but he's only played thirty-one times. How so? Well, he was the *reserve* scrum-half. Forever on the replacements bench behind a chap called George Gregan.

For ten long years, Whitaker faithfully served his country without ever getting the chance to grab a proper place in the spotlight like all his other squad mates. He knew he would *never* get a look in because Gregan was not only the first choice for scrum half but in later years captain as well. Yet year after year, he tried his heart out while never once complaining – or, importantly, white-anting his rival.

Then finally Whitaker *did* get a chance. In 2005 Gregan's form dipped dramatically and everyone – I mean, everyone – said that Whitaker's time had come and he should be selected ahead of Gregan for the upcoming Tri-nation competition. And what did Whitaker do? Yep, he *supported* Gregan. Whitaker became Gregan's most vocal supporter. Astonishing. Behaviour that a good few of our politicians and corporate high-flyers could well learn from.

Whitaker himself would be hideously embarrassed by any such talk. He may be courageous, prodigiously talented, and loyal, but on top of it all he is unfailingly humble, always avoiding any unwarranted attention. Indeed, Whitaker's long-term team mate Morgan Turinui once remarked in awe, 'He's so self-deprecating, it's unbelievable.'

What a hugely refreshing change from the usual cast of supposed heroes we get served up by the media. A friend of mine calls them 'FIGJAMs'. FIGJAM standing for Fuck I'm Good, Just Ask Me.

People need heroes – *I* need heroes – but for society to function properly, I feel it is essential we have the right *type* of heroes. Not the self-centred, one-dimensional FIGJAMs we are so often asked to admire. There is a difference between being an entertainer and being a hero. I find it entertaining to watch many sporting stars perform, but that doesn't mean I admire their failed relationships, raging decadence, or egocentric boasting. Elle Macpherson of all people once wisely remarked of supermodel Kate Moss, 'She's a fashion model, not a role model.' It's a good point.

Chris Whitaker is so unusual – and admirable – precisely because his off-field behaviour is every bit as impressive as his on-field heroics. My sons' local rugby club, the Clovelly Eagles, is a wonderful institution with a motto after my own heart: 'Play to win, learn to lose.' A fabulous sentiment if ever there was one, and an approach many a professional club would do well to adopt. (Yeah, I know, a laughable suggestion in this 'nothing but winning counts' culture.)

Every year, they have a presentation day in one of the area's RSL or surf clubs. It's a chance for the boys and parents to have their moment. There's an award for everything, so no one is left out. Lovely occasions though they are, inevitably the bits where your kids aren't involved are ever so slightly less engaging. It's a successful, thriving club, so each age group has a number of teams. This means it is a long day. A very long day. Few parents stay for the whole thing. Let's just say it's not a spectator sport for a bystander. Which only served to increase my admiration for Chris Whitaker when, a couple of years ago, he was asked to present the awards. *Don't be silly*, I thought. *He's just been selected for the Wallabies' European tour – he's got enough on his plate preparing for his imminent departure. He won't want to be hanging around the Coogee RSL for half his weekend.*

But I was wrong. Whitaker accepted and duly turned up on the day. He actually turned up early, so he was there for the start and the Under 6 teams' presentations. The organisation was friendly but chaotic. Getting people to be quiet was impossible. Whitaker took it all in his stride and shook each of the kids' hands before handing over a medal. *I wonder how long he's going to stay*, I thought. *Don't suppose there's any chance he'll hang around until the Under 8s. Harry would love it if he did.* Unbelievably, he stayed the whole time until it was Harry's team's turn. Harry was thrilled. *Surely, he must go soon*, I thought. *He's been here for hours. He's not getting paid – it's not even like he's getting that much attention.* To cut a long story short, Whitaker stayed not just for Harry's team but for Alex's as well *and* right until the very end. *The whole day, in fact.* Remarkable. At the end, when he eventually left, there wasn't any fanfare – he just shook a few hands and slipped away.

I'm not saying we can all be like Whitaker. I'm sure he can't be as perfect as I believe him to be, either. However, as an ideal to aspire to and learn from – and have our kids learn from – I think you'd be hard-pushed to find better. I suppose what I am saying is that we need to be careful about the people we put on a pedestal. It's as if the only people truly fit to be politicians are the people who don't want to be one. Our heroes might be better chosen from the ranks of those who don't define themselves as heroic. There is a place in this world for over-achieving, ambitious, self-obsessed, stars, but I prefer my heroes to be cut from a different cloth.

Hence my terror that I'll bump into Chris Whitaker one day and discover that he's a FIGJAM after all.

Heaven

I have a good friend and business colleague called Mark. One day last year, we were flying to Melbourne together to give a presentation to an important client. We'd agreed to meet at the airport.

I arrived before him and made myself at home in the business-class lounge. Five minutes later, Mark turned up. He was wearing a coat, carrying a briefcase in one hand and a new paperback in the other. He put the briefcase on the floor and the paperback on the table in front of me so he could take off his coat. I saw the book was Mitch Albom's *The Five People You Meet in Heaven*.

'Bugger. Mate, if only I'd met you ten minutes earlier, I could have saved you thirty bucks,' I said.

'What do you mean?' Mark asked.

'That book. I could have stopped you buying it. It's the worst piece of rubbish that has ever been foisted on mankind. I read it on my last holiday. Pure, unadulterated bollocks. Kept thinking it had to get better, but it only gets worse. Total crap from start to finish.'

'That's a shame,' he replied. 'I bought it for you.'

He picked up the book, opened it at the first page and handed it to me. Inside, I saw he'd written the inscription: 'To Nigel, I hope to meet you there one day. Love, Mark.'

Ouch.

So often, I've unintentionally upset people with my words. People I love. My aunt-in-law is a remarkable lady called Joan. I remember several years back, when Kate and I had just had our first baby, Joan was staying with us in London for a few days, helping Kate get used to the whole motherhood thing. I was working flat-out at the time. One week, after a particularly tough day at the office and a terrible commute on the bus, I came home to find Joan in our sitting room watching the news on TV. I put my briefcase down, kissed her on the cheek and said, 'Hi Joan, where are Kate and the baby? Jesus, could you turn the telly down – it's like an old people's home in here. Can I get you a drink? No? Okay. Catch you in a minute,' and walked upstairs to find Kate.

She wasn't upstairs, so I took the opportunity to change out of my work clothes.

I'd barely got my shirt off before a furious Kate appeared.

'What on earth did you say to Aunty Joan?' she demanded. 'She's downstairs with tears running down her cheeks!'

'Er – nothing. I just said hello and asked her if she wanted a drink.'

Trouble is, that's what I remember saying. I was simply not mindful enough. Open my big fat mouth and let the first words that spring to mind tumble out, that's me. Later that evening, Joan not only repeated to Kate the full version of my comments, she also explained that she had recently been told by her doctor that she was becoming increasingly hard of hearing.

A couple of months ago, my gorgeous six-year-old daughter Grace hugged me and said, 'Mattie is so funny, Daddy – all she does is eat and sleep.'

'Bit like you, sweetheart,' I replied with a smile.

Grace looked at me in an adoringly trusting, questioning way for a moment, then her bottom lip started to quiver and she began crying before running to her mum.

Not good enough. Simply not good enough.

I have a shameful history of similar offences. It's bad enough in direct conversation, but put a phone in my hand and the damage escalates to a different level.

I try to speak to my brother at least once a week. We're a small family and, as I have no other siblings, it's important to me. Given that we live in Australia and he's in the UK, our communication is limited to the phone. Earlier this year, I called him for one of our regular chats.

'Hi, mate,' I opened.

'Hi, Nige,' he replied. 'Glad you called tonight – I've got something I've been wanting to tell you. Some of our friends have been freaked out by the news and sniffily judgemental. I'm a little embarrassed by the whole thing, to be honest. I want you to promise to be open-minded before I tell you –'

'Get on with it, for Christ's sake, John – what's the news?' I interrupted.

'Well, we've got rats –'

'Is that it?' I interrupted again. 'You'll get no sniffiness from us, mate. We've had rats for six months. Kate and I have also been too embarrassed to tell anyone – I'm so glad we're not the only ones. We can't seem to get rid of the little fuckers. They started coming up from behind the cooker. We tried blocking the hole with wood and they simply ate through it. When I blocked it with cement, they found another way in through the air vent. Last week, we found rat droppings in the sink and on the draining board, it's disgusting –'

'Nige?' It was my brother's turn to interrupt.

'Yep?

'When I said "rats", I didn't mean "rat rats", I meant "pet rats",' he explained.

'Oh,' I replied.

'Jack and Ollie were insistent,' he continued. 'Rats are the craze at school. They're actually quite cute – one white, one brown. Wouldn't dream of letting them in the house, of course – they live in a cage at the end of the garden.'

Great.

The lesson I take from this incident isn't so much that I should stop interrupting and let people finish – it's more that I am right to be utterly paranoid about the dangers of using the phone. Long before mobile phones were invented, I've always had a love–hate relationship with the old fixed-line machines. One particular memory still makes me audibly exclaim in painful embarrassment when it involuntarily pops into my mind. Annoyingly, it usually does so in the most inappropriate of circumstances – a business meeting or dinner party – invariably leading people to caringly inquire if I'm all right. I then have to invent an excuse about a headache, stubbed toe, or some such.

Surprisingly, the passing of a considerable number of years has in no way dimmed the pain of this stubborn memory. I had just turned fifteen at the time of the phone call in question and was in a boarding school on the outskirts of Oxford. To my delight, I'd finally found a girl willing to have sex with me more than once. Given my age and my upbringing, this was of course a glorious secret. Her name was Bridget Simpson. Thrillingly, she was two years older than me, adding to the already almost unbearable delirium of proceedings. She lived at home with her parents in the centre of Oxford. It was a short bicycle ride from the school to her place but, being the well-brought-up lad that I was, I always called in advance of a visit to warn of my arrival – and butter up the parents. I was smart enough to realise that keeping Mr and Mrs Simpson sweet was absolutely vital to the continuation of my new-found, and secret, sexual adventure. A little bit of attention in their direction seemed well worth the effort.

I dialled their number from the payphone in the school cafeteria.

Mrs Simpson answered in her friendly but plummy tone.

'Oh hi, Mrs Simpson. It's Nigel,' I said.

'Hello, Nigel. No need for the formality, please do call me Deirdre. Are you coming over to visit us today?' she replied. 'I've made another batch of those scones you seemed to love last weekend.'

'Well, in that case I'll be over straightaway,' I told her. 'I've eaten a lot of scones in my time, but never as nice as the ones you make, Deirdre.'

'Flattery will get you nowhere, Nigel,' she joked.

'Just the truth, Deirdre. I can't thank you enough for how kind you and Brian have been to me. It gets lonely stuck in a boarding school with your family far away in another country. Visiting Bridget and the family is an absolute treat – over the past few weeks, Church Cottage has become like a second home to me.'

'Oh, Nigel, you say the nicest things. Would you like me to fetch Bridget for you? I'll be a moment – I think she's down the bottom of the garden,' she said.

As Mrs Simpson went to get her daughter, I felt a tide of adolescent horniness sweep over me. Thinking about my impending visit and the inevitable clandestine thrills that Bridget and I would soon be sharing made me want to jump on my bike and start peddling right away, rather than wait for her to come to the phone. In fact, now I think of it, she was taking ages. The garden wasn't that big – what the hell was keeping her so long? After what seemed like five minutes, I finally heard Bridget's footsteps on the kitchen flagstones as she approached and picked up the phone.

'Nigel?' she wheezed in an out-of-breath croak.

'Blimey, you sound completely out of breath, you old fuckbox,' I replied. 'My advice to you is to take a rest pretty damn sharpish, as the hard-on I've got in my pants right now is going to take some seriously substantial and sustained shagging before it subsides. I'll be round in forty minutes. Think of an excuse to cut down the parental chit-chat, would you? I don't really want to have to eat a plate of scones and drink a pot of tea before getting your knickers off . . .'

'Nigel, I couldn't find Bridget,' a now slightly less out of breath and hideously frosty Mrs Simpson replied. 'I think she's gone to the shops. I don't think this week is the best time to visit – we're going to be rather busy.'

To my shame, I've 100 such stories I could tell. Teenage howlers and phone faux pas aside, however, I'd just like to make the simple observation that the world would be a whole lot happier, and people would get on a whole lot better, if everyone paused before they spoke to consider the effect their words might have on the people around them. I now attempt to be mindful of my objective when speaking. If, for example, it is to be friendly and jocular – as it was with Mark, Joan and Grace – then I try to pause for a moment to consider if the words I'm about to utter are likely to have the intended effect, or if there is the potential for an entirely contrary outcome. If it's the latter, I've made a promise to myself to err on the side of caution and not say it.

Edamame

Mind you, sometimes not saying it mightn't be the best course of action.

If you asked 100 people how to pronounce the word 'ghoti', I'm confident that at least ninety-nine of them would reply 'got-ee'. A smartarse, however, could point out that it is perfectly logical to pronounce it 'fish'.

It actually *is* pronounced 'fish' – if you take the 'gh' from 'enough', the 'o' from 'women' and the 'ti' from 'nation'. Try it.

Luckily, we all seem to share the unspoken belief that it is 'got-ee' and you'd be a dickhead to insist on pronouncing it 'fish'. The world would simply stop functioning unless most of us knew, and agreed on, what to do in the majority of situations.

I, too, pronounce it 'got-ee'. I haven't got a problem with ninety-nine per cent of the situations I encounter. It's the one per cent that trips me up. Over the past forty-odd years, I have constantly struggled with the accepted norms of behaviour in those 'marginal' areas of modern life. It's not so much that I rebel against them, it's more that half the time it is so damn hard to know what the accepted norms *are*.

To take an example from my business career – pathetic though it may be to admit – I've always been crippled with doubt about how to behave in those 'senior client comes and stands next to you at the urinal' moments. I've some friends who jump straight in and strike up a conversation as if they haven't got their dick in their hands, while I know others who take the 'refuse to acknowledge his existence' approach. It's a bit of a Hobson's choice, if you ask me, as each option is equally problematic. Ignoring someone's presence when they're standing barely two inches away from you strikes me as a little bit odd if your relationship with him normally involves bowing and scraping. But then again, if he is genuinely senior, it's natural to feel that certain boundaries are appropriate.

Just as you don't pat the Queen on the arse (unless you're Paul Keating) I can understand why the client himself might prefer not to be spoken to while he shakes his penis. I tend to veer towards the 'ignore' camp, as I've a feeling that the line has to be drawn somewhere else we will all soon be having business conversations through the stall doors while we wipe our arses. I just want to do the right thing, however, and wish someone would tell me what it was, either way.

I still shudder at the thought of one 'marginal' occasion where, in retrospect, I clearly made the wrong decision. I was at dinner in London with the CEO of our largest client. It was a family-run firm, and Susan, the matriarch, had overcome extreme hardship and an extraordinarily humble country upbringing in Yorkshire to successfully set up and run a multimillion-dollar company. As such, my guest was rightly used to being treated with an element of respect.

I liked her enormously and always enjoyed our meetings, but it would be fair to say she did have a slight chip on her shoulder about her humble roots and rural existence. She clearly relished these trips to London to visit her advertising agency. It was a chance both to enjoy the 'sophisticated' London high life and to prove she was comfortable in it. The unspoken assumption was always that I would book the swankiest new restaurant in town, and this time I'd excelled myself by securing the best table at the latest hideously expensive and exclusive Japanese restaurant on Hyde Park.

She was thrilled when we walked in – 'Oh, well done, Nigel – perfect,' she said.

I've always adored Japanese food and, when she asked me to order for us both, I took real pleasure in choosing a variety of dishes that I thought would give her an enjoyable experience.

As we waited for our food, a waiter approached the table and informed me that I had an urgent call. Susan was charm itself and insisted I should take it.

It was indeed a rather urgent call and, despite my best efforts to make it as short as possible, I was away from the table for at least ten minutes. On my return, I made profuse apologies only to have Susan wave them away pleasantly, saying, 'No problem at all, Nigel, don't even mention it. I've been enjoying my surroundings – and besides, no sooner had you left than they brought me these.'

I looked at the table and, to my horror, saw an enormous bowl *half full* of edamame beans. As I sat down, Susan reached in, picked up a bean and popped it whole into her mouth.

'I do apologise, but I think I've eaten over half already. They are rather tasty. Stringy, but tasty,' she said. 'You have the rest.'

Now, it was at this moment that I needed someone to tell me what the accepted norm would be in this situation. She clearly had no idea that you were supposed to suck the beans out of the shells and place the shells in the saucer next to the bowl. I suddenly suspected she hadn't been to a Japanese restaurant before. She was eating them whole – revolting shells and all. I debated telling her the correct way of eating them but decided it would be simply too mortifying for her. Although I didn't mind in the slightest, I was certain that to explain would play to her deepest fears and make her feel I was showing her up as an unsophisticated out-of-towner. I debated eating them in the right way in front of her and letting her work it out herself, but that seemed just as bad, if not worse. I even debated saying I was 'full', but that was a bloody stupid idea given that we hadn't eaten anything yet. Finally, I toyed with the idea of telling her I didn't actually like edamame, but as I'd just personally ordered them a few minutes ago, that didn't strike me as believable or sensible, either. Instead, I made what now seems the absurdly stupid decision of finishing the bowl exactly as she had started it – shells and all. To this day, I don't know how I managed not to be sick. 'Stringy' didn't quite catch it – 'gopping', more like it. It's not a culinary experience I look back on fondly.

It may have saved the evening, but it has permanently ruined my reaction to edamame. In retrospect, this is one occasion where I feel I should have pointed out it was indeed 'got-ee', not 'fish'.

iPod

The woman who pulled up at my booth was clearly approaching the end of her tether. She had four young children in soccer regalia in the back of her car and all appeared to be screaming, shouting or crying. Despite her best efforts to control them, she wasn't having any success. I gave her a sympathetic look as I took her order.

'I've got four myself,' I said as supportively as possible. 'Can be a right handful sometimes.'

'Oh, I'm so sorry for the noise,' she replied anxiously.

'No worries. Yours are positively angelic, compared with mine. Don't mention it – we're here to help.'

'Yeah, the Happy Meal toys seem to be the only thing that shuts them up,' she said.

I was manning the drive-through booth at McDonald's to get a better understanding of how our latest client worked. Leo Burnett was winning business – big business – and one of our major wins was McDonald's. In my industry, this was a big deal. In my company, this was a HUGE deal. You see, Leo Burnett have worked for McDonald's for a number of decades around the world. But for the thirty-odd years that McDonald's have been operating in Australia, Leo Burnett had never got a look-in – however hard they'd attempted to get a slice of the action. And trust me, they had tried. Hard.

The win was all the more exciting because McDonald's had a visionary new CEO, Peter Bush, who was determined to radically change and improve the company. It was precisely the type of situation that suited our firm – and me.

In a new relationship such as this, one of the first things any decent ad agency has to do is get to know the operations of its new partner. At the coalface, not just in the boardroom. Depending on the type of company it is, this might mean visiting the distillery, touring with the door-to-door sales reps or flying with the airline.

Whatever gives you a real insight into the fabric of their organisation. In McDonald's case, it obviously involved working in their restaurants. Now, I know some CEOs who regard this type of thing as an unfortunate 'duty' to be delegated to underlings. I take a contrary view. Leaving aside the fact that I actually *like* doing them, I feel it is essential for sound business reasons that the top brass are forced to leave their ivory tower and undertake these assignments.

McDonald's couldn't have been more helpful in accommodating our desire to work in one of their restaurants. It must be a right pain to have a couple of bumbling idiots from head office getting in your way when you've got an enormously busy restaurant to run, but the young employees were as helpful and welcoming as it was humanly possible to be.

Throughout the morning, my colleague and I were given a variety of different tasks to do or shadow. At lunchtime, once we were slightly more familiar with how things worked, we were each allocated a job to do for the rest of the day.

Mine was the drive-through. I found it quite tricky to start with. We were in the busiest outlet in Sydney at the busiest time, so you had to move at a rapid pace else you jammed up the whole system behind you. The complexity of the number of different orders and buttons took a bit of getting used to. After half an hour of practice, however – and some patient and expert tuition from the frighteningly bright and charming sixteen-year-old whose shift I was buggering up – I started to get the hang of it.

Now, my mother has always claimed I've got a short attention span. My brother phrases it differently, saying I am 'a great starter but an awful finisher'. Personally, I'd appreciate a bit more support from my immediate family, but there might just be an element of truth in their views. I do love a challenge – I find the whole process of getting to know a new situation and figuring out how to change or improve it energising and exciting. The only bit I like more is the next bit. The *doing* bit. That initial stage where your learning – and (hopefully) impact – is at its greatest. It gives me a rush that I find incredibly rewarding. Once the initial stage is over, however, and you enter 'maintenance mode', my passion and enthusiasm do tend to come off the boil a bit. Luckily for me, I find this initial process can sometimes last for years, enabling me to hold down a number of rewarding long-term jobs in my career. On other occasions, though, the initial process lasts only a few hours – and when it does, my mind has a tendency to search for ways to spice things up a little bit. Needless to say, not always with the desired outcome.

Forty-five minutes into my drive-through job, I began to feel confident. An hour in, and the novelty started to wear off. Two hours in, I was bored. Three, and I was going out of my mind – and I still had two hours to go. My respect for the people who do these jobs day in, day out and still retain a friendly and professional attitude reached new heights. I felt guilty at my restlessness. I wasn't used to days like this. I was used to more variety, more interaction, more fun.

The drive-through traffic had been non-stop. For the past hour, most of the custom had been from harassed mums with young kids in the car on their way home after school sport. I know how hideous the kids' dinner-time end-of-day rush can be, and I was gaining a valuable insight into how welcome it is for a parent to be able to drive quickly in and out of McDonald's in the late afternoon and have dinner sorted without the need for any cooking or washing. The look of relief on the mums' faces when I handed over their kids' meals was actually quite moving. They knew that they would now, for ten minutes at least, actually have some well-deserved peace and quiet.

Serving these mums involved not just taking and fulfilling their order. It also involved asking them which colour toy they would like in their Happy Meal box.

The Happy Meal toys were in two crates on the floor of the booth – one filled with flimsy cheap plastic pink toys, the other with flimsy cheap plastic blue toys. Upon being told the colour of preference, I would bend down, pick up the appropriate toy and put it in the Happy Meal box before closing it and handing over the completed order to the waiting mum.

'What colour would you like?' I asked this particularly harassed-looking mother of four, bending down to the crates to get them. We'd agreed that the Happy Meal toys were a saving grace.

'Two pink and two blue, please. By the way, what are they today?' she asked.

'iPods,' I replied.

Now, bear with me. It seemed like a witty, charming, ironic . . . oh, let's just say I was bored and it seemed like a good idea at the time. I was genuinely trying to be friendly and lighten the mood.

'Kids!!!!' she immediately exclaimed before I even had a chance to get up from beneath the counter where the crates were, let alone explain that I was joking. 'It's iPods today! IPODS! We're going to get iPods!!! I know I said we couldn't afford one. Well, now you're *each* going to have one all of your own. You'd better take care of them. And be sure to thank the nice man.'

Oh, lordy.

The nice man couldn't think of a clever way out of this self-created mess – so he chose cowardice instead. The next car was waiting. I know it's not an excuse, but I was under pressure . . .

'Have a nice day,' I said as I deceitfully handed over four iPodless Happy Meal boxes to the now pathetically grateful-looking mum.

As the rush-hour traffic hurried her through the drive-through lane, I could hardly bring myself to think about the mayhem she was about to unleash when she handed over the boxes and they discovered the truth. Or indeed what I was about to do to her faith in human nature.

Wherever you are, I can only apologise.

Nelson Mandela

The iPod incident highlights an important lesson about my personality – and one of its long-running central flaws. Namely, humour. Or, more accurately, my attempts at humour. Looking back, I can recall numerous occasions when my humour has misfired and upset people rather than entertained or relaxed them. It isn't that I can't be funny and entertain – it's more that I have a tendency to thoughtlessly choose the wrong time or the wrong audience or the wrong story in my humorous forays. I blame stand-up comedy.

I can clearly remember the very first time I went to a stand-up night. It was in the early 1980s in central London, at a place called The Comedy Store. Stand-up was just beginning to take off and was being written about as the new rock'n'roll. The gig started at midnight. This was during my drinking days, so by that time of night I was extremely well oiled – as was the rest of the audience. The place was packed and intimidating. It must have been a terrifying spot to perform. These late-night gigs had started to get a bit of a reputation. Things regularly got thrown at the performers. Heckling was frequent and aggressive. Fights, not just between audience members but between performers and the audience, were common. Just as punk was a shock and an affront to pop, stand-up was a welcome change from, and slap in the face to, a boring night out at the theatre or cinema. I was excited just waiting for the acts to start. It somehow felt dangerous to be sitting near the front as the comedians were known to pick on individual audience members as part of their act.

After ten minutes, and an extra couple of swift pints on my part, the MC came on stage and said, 'We've got a great line-up tonight, so we're going to get started straightaway . . . after this important safety notice.' He held up a bit of paper and read, 'This venue was designed to hold fifty people. In the event of a fire, panic like fuck as there are no emergency exits and we've sold 200 tickets, all to people who are completely shit-faced.' He then screwed up the bit of paper into a ball, kicked it into the audience and shouted, 'Ladies and gentlemen, put your hands together for our first act – Jerry Sadowitz!' With this, he ran off stage. After a brief pause, Sadowitz walked on. He looked like Punch out of Punch and Judy. He was wearing a flat cap perched on a huge head of curly dark hair. Without any introduction, he walked to the mike, levelly eyeballed the crowd and calmly said (and I'm quoting verbatim here), 'Nelson Mandela – what a cunt.'

Now, I feel I need to explain that at this time Mandela was still in jail. Moreover, to the circles I moved in, and in particular to the type of crowd I was part of, he was a god. If not God. In the UK, this was the era when there were regular marches, attended by thousands, protesting that the South African government 'free Nelson Mandela'. There was even a song in the top ten of the pop charts of that very name. Mandela was *the* most revered figure of the time. It would be difficult to exaggerate what an outrageous thing it was for Sadowitz to say. It must have been a bit like when Nietzsche declared that 'God is dead' in 1882. Except when Nietzsche said it, he was actually writing it in a book, not saying it on a stage in front of 200 very drunk, rowdy people. Quite apart from the blasphemy to Mandela, the use of the 'C word' was also utterly shocking. This was in the days when the F word still had the power to offend and appall – and, as a result, was used sparingly, if at all. No one, and I mean no one, used the C word in public. Ever. The immediacy and intimacy of the venue served to heighten the effect. The people in the front row were jammed up against the stage and could reach out and touch, or punch, the performers without even having to take a step forward.

So all in all to walk on stage that night and calmly announce 'Nelson Mandela – what a cunt' was a pretty remarkable thing to do. And witness. Indeed, I've never forgotten it. But it was his follow-up line that really had the impact. He waited for a couple of seconds, to let the shock and outrage settle into the crowd, then leant into the microphone and said in an irritated and conspiratorial voice, 'I mean, you lend some people five bucks and you don't see them again for twenty years. Typical.'

The effect was truly magical. The place exploded in an uproar of laughter. The collective relief from the crowd that he had pricked the tension by following up his opening line with a joke – and that it was funny – was palpable. The individual effect was slightly more messy, as I snorted beer out of my nose, I was laughing so hard. From there, Sadowitz just kept coming at the audience like a steam train. It was a marvellous, exhilarating, awe-inspiring performance. I was hooked and spent the next ten years going to stand-up as often as I could.

Obviously, you had to be there but Sadowitz's joke reinforces the lesson from my iPod story, a lesson it's taken me more than twenty years to learn. Humour has to be appropriate to your audience and situation. What is acceptable to a drunken bunch of adults who've chosen to go to a comedy venue is not necessarily acceptable in a sermon in church on a Sunday. It may seem obvious when I use such an extreme example, but it's when the situations are less extreme that I have found it more difficult to stay on 'the right side' of the line.

The management consultants McKinsey & Company apparently have an acronym, GAME, which they use when preparing for a big presentation. It stands for Goal, Audience, Message, Expression. I wish someone had told me about it earlier. Sadowitz's goal was to make a group of people laugh, his audience a drunk, young, edgy comedy crowd, his message a topical joke and therefore his memorable expression of it was arguably justified.

Too often in my past I have been guilty of using humour which in a different situation would have been fine, but in the one in which I used it was simply inappropriate. My intention with the 'iPod mum' was to brighten her day with a jovial remark. My impact, however, was most likely to fuck up her day. There is an important point here, and this point goes far beyond simply humour – it covers all behaviour.

My observation is this: in many ways, intentions are irrelevant when it comes to your behaviour. It is your *impact* on other people that is the crucial thing. It's not an adequate defence to say 'I was just trying to be funny' if your impact is in reality to be offensive or hurtful. I've become increasingly mindful that I have a responsibility to be aware of my likely impact upon other people.

I only recently realised with a shock, for example, that my excitement at and enjoyment of describing whatever I'm currently doing could in certain circles come across as 'showing off', rather than 'loving to share'. Initially, I was angry and hurt by this notion – why shouldn't I be pleased and keen to talk about the speech (or whatever) I've just done?

'Because it is off-putting and makes you appear a big-headed arse, that's why,' is Kate's helpful answer.

As a result of her input, I went to a recent family gathering determined to say nothing about myself. At all. Remarkably (to Kate, anyway), I succeeded, and it was the nicest, most relaxed occasion I can remember. Surprisingly, I also enjoyed it far more than any of the other occasions where I had felt the need to tell everyone else what I was doing at the time.

It's a lesson Kate irritatingly points out she wished I would implement more at home . . .

Mrs Marsh

I find that poor communication skills are often at the heart of so many of the issues I struggle with. Bizarrely, though, it often seems harder to communicate with people the *closer* they are to you.

There was one occasion soon after we moved to Australia when my mum so upset me on the phone that, unbeknown to Kate, I took the brand new cordless handset I'd been using out into the garden after the conversation had finished, placed it on the patio floor and stamped on it. Violently and repeatedly – until my right knee started to hurt so much that I had to stop. We'd just bought a fancy new base station with two cordless handsets to better enable us to talk on the phone while looking after our four young kids. It had cost an eye-watering sum, so I felt ever so slightly guilty at having flattened one of them so soon after buying it. But at least we had another.

Kate came downstairs and into the kitchen. 'Sweetheart, I'm so sorry, I've just dropped one of the handsets in the bath while washing Evie. It's totally buggered. I can't get it to make a noise, let alone work. I'm so, so sorry – I know it was expensive. We'll just have to make do with one handset,' she said. 'Where is the other one, by the way? I was on the phone to Dad when I dropped it and I need to call him back.'

'In the garden,' I weakly replied.

My mum and I don't just have an issue with telephone communication – there is also the not inconsiderable matter of getting on face to face.

We've probably had to do it less than most families, given my early departure to boarding school and my subsequent decision to emigrate to Australia. However, since my dad's illness and move to a nursing home, Kate and I have been seeing more of Mum in the flesh, as she tends to visit at least once a year. Last year was no exception. Mum came out for a whole month over Christmas.

It's the third time she has come out by herself and the visit followed a predictable 'relationship rhythm'.

To start with, the air crackled with tension. Mum is a lovely, caring and well-mannered guest but I always felt she had this way of *radiating* disapproval. She didn't need to say anything, or do anything – she simply radiated the fact that she thought our children's table manners were disgusting. Just by raising an eyebrow, she could communicate that she thought the house was a mess, *she* wouldn't cook pasta like that and that we were bringing our kids up to be terrorists. Apparently, there's a scientific term for it – metacommunication. Well, I'd decided that Mum was a metacommunicator par excellence.

The simplest of conversations took on the richest complexity.

'We're all going to the park, Mum,' I would say. 'Would you like to come?'

'Yes,' Mum would reply, all the while radiating *No*.

Cleverly picking up on this metacommunication, I would say, 'Only come if you want to, Mum. It's very relaxed. We're happy either way.'

'No, I'd like to come,' she'd reply, radiating the very opposite.

She'd then sit in the park looking like she was sucking a particularly bitter lemon, and I'd spend the whole time constantly looking over at her, worrying about what she was thinking.

An amazing thing happened after two weeks, however. Everyone just seemed to relax. Conversations became easier. The tension disappeared. One Saturday, Mum came down to watch the family compete in the swim club at the Bronte Beach pool – and it was delightful. She charmed everyone. I then took the hitherto unthinkable step of asking her if she would like to come to the Quakers with me the next day. Attending the Quakers is something I have come to late in life. With the demands of four young children, I find it hard to go as often as I would like, but when I do go, I find it of enormous value. To invite someone else to come with me on one of the rare occasions I had the chance to attend was a big deal. Especially asking my mum. It had all the hallmarks of being a stupid idea. Quaker 'meetings' couldn't be more different from the church services Mum usually attends. Basically, at the Quakers, you go and sit in silence for an hour. The potential for her to hate it and me to feel awkward and have my experience ruined was, on a scale of one to two – two. To my surprise, though, she said she'd love to come with me, in a way that seemed to communicate that she *would* love to. Even more surprising, when we went we had a fabulous time – before, during and after.

It became a virtuous circle – we did ever more things together in an ever more enjoyable, comfortable and close way. On the day before she was due to fly back to the UK, I took her to the movies at Mrs Macquarie's Chair. This is one of Sydney's famous outdoor cinema venues during the summer. The cinema screen literally is *in* the harbour – in the water itself. If that isn't enough, the backdrop is the gorgeously lit Sydney skyline, Harbour Bridge and Opera House. It has to be a pretty good movie to compete with the view. Luckily, this time it was. Halfway through the film, I felt Mum put her head on my shoulder. Walking back to the car afterwards, she put her arm around me and I responded in kind. Over the last forty-four years, it was the closest I think I have ever been to my mum. I really didn't want her to go.

Driving back from the airport the next day, having dropped her off for her flight, I reflected on her stay and my feelings. I concluded that all that stuff about Mum being a metacommunicator was bullshit. Communication is a two-way process. Possibly, just possibly, it was me not her who brought the tension and complexity to the table. Maybe it was my neuroses and paranoia that muddied the relationship waters, and it was me who needed to relax.

It reminded me of the time I accused my brother of being a seething bed of latent anger, or some such.

My brother's wife, Celia, had laughed in a kindly way and said, 'Nonsense, Nigel. It's you who's got the anger.'

Bugger me if she wasn't right. It's so much easier to find faults in others than recognise them in yourself – and, more importantly, then face up to them.

On that drive home, I realised that for far too long I had been hideously unfair to my parents. I was ever ready to play the 'woe is me – I was sent to boarding school as a toddler' card. I even wrote a book about it asking them what on earth they had been thinking to send me away.

Who the hell did I think I was? Exactly as we are currently trying to do with Alex, Harry, Grace and Eve, my parents were just doing the best they could with what they had at the time. Parenting is hard. To my mind, there is too much advice and analysis out there that serves to make people feel bad about the job they are doing as parents or feel like a victim because of the job their own parents did. We are all making it up as we go – no one has all the answers or the monopoly on the right way. It's all just *opinion*. And your personal opinion is pretty valid, however unsure you feel about the job you're doing as a parent and a role model. I have never admitted this before but in hindsight, while I don't agree with it, I can fully understand my parents' boarding school decision.

As I arrived home, I had another surprising revelation. When we decided to move to Australia, we had been concerned that it would mean we'd become too distant and removed from our families. The fact of the matter is, we have become dramatically *closer*. Being so far away means that visits have to be of a certain length, so a bizarre by-product of us moving 20,000 kilometres away is that we have spent more time together with my parents than at any time since before I went to school. Not that I need another reason to love the country, but a pleasing realisation nevertheless.

The Seven-day Challenge

As I've worked on my own pitiful imperfections as a communicator, I've started to become more sensitive to, and aware of, how people – and couples in particular – speak to each other. It can be awfully depressing if you monitor it. It's one thing never to praise your partner, but quite another if all you do is fill the void with what I call 'ball-cutting'.

Jill Craigie, the famous British film director and leading feminist, maintained that 'for a marriage to have any chance, every day at least six things should go unsaid'. All the more interesting advice, given that she was happily married for fifty years.

I swear there are times when Kate can go an entire day in which her repertoire of comments to me consists solely of corrections, contradictions and criticisms. The 'three Cs', as I now call them. I know I can be an irritating bastard, but cut me a break, why don't you? Another friend of mine, Matthew, has a phrase that I love – 'let that one go through to the keeper'. I think we'd all rub along better if, when someone said something slightly inaccurate or something we disagreed with, every now and then we let it go through to the keeper and kept our mouth shut. I'm not advocating being a doormat or becoming a sappy, unopinionated church mouse – but rather, a pause to think about what you might be like to live with. I spoke to a dear friend of mine about this and, to my horror, after a couple of minutes' thought, *she burst into tears.*

When I'd calmed her down, she claimed she couldn't remember the last time she had said anything nice to her husband. 'I love him and don't mean to be horrible, Nigel, but I don't know – I just get so tired and life is so busy and he can be so useless that I can't help myself. We end up sniping away at each other. Never giving an inch.'

In a case like this, I believe that being more sparing with your criticism and more generous with your praise can potentially have a wonderfully transformative effect. In this spirit, I asked her to consider trying to go for a week where each day she forced herself to do two simple things. The first was to bite her lip on *one* (only one, not six, like Jill Craigie recommends) occasion when she felt herself about to 'ball-cut' her husband, and say nothing instead. The second was to force herself to say one (only one) nice thing to him on a different occasion within the same day. Irrespective of how he behaved and irrespective of how she felt. If that meant faking it, fine – fake it. AA have a phrase – 'fake it till you make it', which springs to mind here.

Be fake-nice just once within a 24-hour period. Put like that, it doesn't seem all that much to ask, does it?

If doing such a small thing for such a small time sticks in your gut so much that you can't bring yourself to try it, I suggest you take a long, hard look at the person you have become. I simply don't buy into the hard-arsed notion that such an experiment is demeaning or 'threatening to one's sense of self', as one person memorably suggested to me. The worst that can happen is nothing happens. You can always go back and resume normal service, so to speak, the next week.

What happened in this case is that my friend and her husband had the best week they could remember. It created an atmosphere of generosity, not meanness. He was dramatically nicer to her. In return, she was even nicer. And so it went on. Apparently, they even had sex.

This is not a 'women should be nicer to men' thing. It's a 'people should be nicer to people' thing. It's as if a whole section of society now believes that gender equality means having to engage in a perpetual point-scoring competition about who did what household chore. Or, worse, that every conversation is really an opportunity to indulge in a bout of tedious sexual politics. Somehow, virtues such as kindness, gentleness, courtesy, consideration and plain old-fashioned niceness don't get a look in, as we're all too busy fighting in some stupid battle of the sexes.

A twice-divorced friend of mine maintains that deciding to get married or not 'is a choice between a lifetime of loneliness and a lifetime of irritation'. Sadly, he touches on a truth, as all too evidently many marriages are little more than seething beds of resentment and frustration. However, I simply refuse to believe that they have to be.

At the risk of giving self-help-style advice, I can't see how trying this 'one nice thing, one unsaid thing' seven-day challenge once could possibly do any couple any harm.

Basic instinct

Successful communication in marriage is challenging enough when the subject matter is everyday, non-controversial topics – throw sex into the mix and the potential for misunderstanding is taken to a whole new level.

Since the publication of my first book, I've received countless letters from readers regaling me with their stories about the differences in perspective and attitude that exist between them and their partner concerning sex. In return, I thought it only fair I share a story of my own that illustrates the very same point . . .

It happened last year. I was putting a note in the kitchen diary when I suddenly realised it had been three years since I'd lost my excess weight – around 20 kilos in all. Unlike with those pointless yo-yo diets, I had managed to keep the weight off ever since – a fact I was quietly proud of. Despite this success, Kate, as usual, had kept me grounded by constantly needling me about the lack of six-pack, or indeed any muscle definition, on my now slender frame. I made the decision there and then that I would surprise her by secretly going on a muscle-building and toning program. From that day on, I started a regular clandestine schedule of crunches, weights and sit-ups. Two weeks into my regimen, Kate had family news that meant she had to travel to Europe without me – for six weeks. I would no longer have to train in secret! I decided to up the ante while she was gone to maximise the effect on her return. Three weeks into her trip, my schedule was really starting to pay dividends when I got another stroke of luck. An email arrived from one of the firm's overseas offices requesting that I do a farewell video for a departing colleague. Naked.

The idea was that as I was sending my best wishes to the departing Barry, the camera would start on a close-up of my face and, as I spoke, slowly pan back to reveal that I was actually sitting in the office stark bollock naked (it was an in-joke – again, it seemed like a good idea at the time). The prospect of being seen naked on film gave me just the added incentive I needed to really step up my regimen of sculpting an impressive new torso. The effects of my training to date were most apparent on my stomach, so I decided to put special focus on that area over the remaining three weeks before the video was to be filmed – and Kate's return. Every day, I would do curl-downs, sit-ups, leg raises, crunches – every and any exercise I could think of that would tone my tummy. As the day of filming grew nearer, I drove myself even harder, doing literally hundreds of exercises a day. Even though I say it myself, when I finally stripped down to be filmed, I didn't look half bad – no six-pack, but definitely signs of a four-pack.

To minimise potential embarrassment to staff and clients, the filming was done in the company kitchen. I made a point of secretly and ferociously tensing my stomach whenever the camera was on. Later that evening, when I looked at the tape at home, I was delighted – the combination of the six weeks of training, my conscientious tensing and the flattering lighting made my stomach look fit enough to grace the cover of one of those *Men's Health* magazines. I couldn't wait to show Kate.

As always, the London to Sydney flight landed extremely early – 5:10am, to be precise. It would be a long day indeed before we'd strip off for bed and I could reveal my brand new bod. It was wonderful to see Kate again after so long apart. We went for our traditional reunion breakfast at Bronte Beach, followed by a walk to Bondi and back. As we returned to the house, I suddenly had a thought – *rather than wait for bedtime to reveal my four-pack, maybe I could show her the video instead.*

I waited for an appropriate moment then casually said, 'Sweetheart – after lunch, remind me to show you a video we've done for Barry in the London office. It's hysterical. All his mates from each office around the world filmed a short goodbye clip to him – 100 per cent nude. They're going to show it at his leaving party next week.'

'Totally naked?' Kate asked, a gleam in her eyes.

'As the day they were born,' I replied.

'Including you?' Kate said.

'Yep.'

'No way! You must have had something on,' she insisted.

'Not a stitch. It was bloody chilly,' I told her, somewhat unnecessarily.

'Lunch can wait – this I've got to see,' she said. 'Chuck it in the machine now!'

Fabulous – just the response I was after. I put the tape in the machine, grabbed the remote and sat on the sofa next to Kate. I was absurdly excited about the prospect of her reaction at seeing my hard-earned, transformed and rippling torso.

As the tape got to my part, Kate leant forward a bit. Right on cue, just at the point when the camera panned back to reveal my full-frontal, Kate elbowed me in the ribs.

'Nigel, I can't believe it!' she exclaimed.

'What?' I innocently, but smugly, replied.

'That,' she said, pointing at the screen with the remote and pressing the pause button.

'What?' I repeated, this time unable to keep a self-satisfied smile from my face.

'That. There. Behind you. It's one of those American double-door fridges I've been going on about. If we bought one through the company, do you think we'd get a discount?'

Are you one of those couples whose sexual desires are exactly compatible? Do you have it four times a week in an exciting, surprising and rewarding way? Does each of you look forward to it and initiate it as often as the other?

Thought not.

If you *are* one of the above couples, then please feel free to skip the rest of this chapter. Because I'm talking here to the *other people*. The people for whom sex is more a source of tension and stress in their relationship than one of delight and joy.

It's so damn difficult to write about, however. You run the risk of either offending people or appearing foolish in front of the masses who collude in the common lie that everyone is at it like rabbits.

Ever since my first book was published, men have been contacting me saying they love their partner but their sex life is a disaster. Bizarrely, they feel comfortable telling me their innermost thoughts about sex yet they can't tell their partners. Or they can, but never in a way that has the desired effect.

What I thought I'd do, therefore, is anonymously give a flavour of what these men (over 700 of them, to date) say. They say they do love their partners but are permanently sexually frustrated. Their wives never initiate sex.

Instead, as one said, they 'dispense' it. Sex is used as a weapon, a tool with which to leverage power.

Others claim that their wives' goal appears to be to get away with as little sex as they possibly can. It is never planned, as that would be 'unromantic'. Instead, the 'circumstances have to be right' trick is employed to devastating effect. One husband told me Halley's comet comes round more often than the circumstances being right. Seeing as these circumstances involve her not being tired, feeling up for it, feeling 100 per cent comfortable with her weight, it being the right time of the month, there being nothing to worry about with the kids' schools, it not being planned, her husband not 'expecting it', et cetera, et cetera, you can see his point.

Many of these men believe that their wives live in a *willing* state of denial. In their hearts, they know their husbands aren't satisfied with boring, grudgingly dispensed sex once every three weeks, but they'd rather not talk about it. Because then they might have to do something about it. But then again, they know these men aren't going to be unfaithful, so actually there is no real pressing need to do anything about it. They can just live in a permanent state of dissatisfaction – 'overworked and underlaid', as one reader memorably described it in his letter to me.

In summary, these men believe their wives simply *don't care enough*.

Now, as I reread the above, I can imagine the criticism it will provoke. Thing is, I know this is just one very specific point of view. I realise women have a different perspective. I've had hundreds of conversations where friends have described what the issue is like from the point of view of a woman who has kids. They explain how they used to want and enjoy sex when they first married – before children – but that life has since worn them down and circumstances drained them of desire.

'Quite frankly, Nigel, it's just another chore in my already crowded day,' one friend told me. 'I spend all day looking after three kids. When I've finally put them to bed, I have to clean the house, do the laundry and make the packed lunches. Then I cook the dinner. Then the phone usually goes and I have to listen to my mother bleating on about some or other complaint. When I finally get to bed and my husband starts grabbing me, I can't help but push him away in irritation. I don't want to do anything else for anyone else at that time. I just want to be left alone to relax.'

Other women tell me how their husbands have let themselves go, are no longer the man they married. The once fit, charming and caring lover has become a fat, hairy, inconsiderate and emotionally unavailable slob. Others say that they themselves no longer feel special, feminine or sexy. Another friend told me, 'I spend all my life giving to other people. Emotionally giving. All day long. I give to the kids, I give to the school, I give to my friends, I give to my family, I even give to the bloody dog. Give give give. I know I'm probably being stupidly self-sacrificing, but at the end of the day I'm not only physically spent, I'm emotionally spent. Sex with my husband just seems another form of giving and I haven't got anything left to give.' The list goes on. All of them totally human and perfectly understandable.

But bear with me. Try to suspend judgement for just a couple of minutes and imagine there was a situation where there was a loving, loyal, faithful husband. On average, he was having sex once every three weeks. I know it's easier not to delve into the situation, but you needn't ask him – I'm *telling* you, he is not happy. Now, the woman in this situation has a choice – she can carry on with the status quo, as the vast majority of men who've written to me say their partners have done. Or she can do something about it.

But do what?

People are at a loss what to *do*. Well, I've got a radical suggestion. It's based on hundreds of interviews. It's something I've never seen fail. And it's free.

It's also simple to implement.

Bonk him more.

That's it. Bonk him more.

I'm serious. Plan for there to be just a few extra 'special cuddles' in your life.

No, don't try to arrange circumstances so you'll want it more often – you won't.

Equally, don't try to arrange circumstances so he'll want it less – he won't.

Just make the decision to bonk him more. Regularly.

I'm not talking about doing it every day or doing anything painful or illegal. I'm talking about, let's say, having sex *once a week*. We seem to live in a society where it's an unspeakable thought to suggest that a woman have sex with her partner when she doesn't want to. Of course, in every other situation than the one I'm talking about, it is. But don't hide behind that fact. Stick to the situation I'm talking about. Doesn't being part of a loving couple mean prioritising your partner's sexual satisfaction? It's naive to believe that good, loving, regular sex is written in the stars and just happens when he jumps off his horse, swims across the lake – still in his full military uniform, of course – and sweeps you into his arms. In its way, this is just as immature as the clichéd fantasy men have of their women being anything like the open-mouthed, bikini-clad nymphomaniacs portrayed in lads' mags. Ideal fantasies and week-to-week reality are unlikely to bear any resemblance, and people need to be able to distinguish between the two if the latter is going to have any chance of being consistently joyful.

Much as this view will get me into trouble, I feel there are a number of women out there who quite frankly are just a little lazy and thoughtless when it comes to their husband's sexual needs. Please resist the understandable temptation to resort to the non sequitur of 'women have had to put up with unsatisfactory sex lives for centuries'. Why that fact would somehow make it all right to ignore your husband's needs today is beyond me.

Knowing your husband is desperate for more regular sex and not doing anything about it while hoping he won't mention it isn't really good enough, to my mind. Ridiculing him for his desires and frustration takes spite to a whole new level. I've lost count of the number of times I've heard women talk about their husband's sexual needs in a jokey, disparaging way to their friends. 'Oh, John always wants sex during the day – I simply *have* to make sure I'm out of the house when he comes back at lunch.' Ho bloody ho.

I spent fifteen unsuccessful years trying to give up drink. Circumstances never seemed right. *If only I could sort out all the other issues in my life, then I'll get round to giving up the booze*, I used to think. Then, one day, I realised I'd got it the wrong way round – I needed to give up the drink to be *able* to sort out the other issues. I gave up drink rather than wait for the right time to give up drink. Blow me if the other issues didn't go and sort themselves out shortly after.

In many cases, it's the same with sex. *There are just so many other issues we need to sort out in our relationship before we can have sex*, women tell the men who have written to me. Well, maybe and maybe not. You might find that having sex will actually *help* you fix those other issues.

Besides, if you had more sex, there's a chance you might find you enjoyed it. It might make you closer as a couple. It might become a vital part of what makes your union special. It could reconnect you. It could be a glorious source of tenderness, intimacy and naughtiness. It is, after all, the only thing that is exclusive to the two of you. You laugh with other people, eat with other people, watch films with other people . . . You could find yourself in an entirely new relationship dynamic. Where physical closeness leads to emotional closeness, rather than the other way round. Where you start looking forward to it as a highlight of your week. If you don't, well, the worst thing that could happen is you make your partner happier and you have sex once a week when you'd rather not.

I've talked to many women who've tried the 'have more sex' approach. Without exception, they've told me their relationship has improved out of sight. They didn't feel like prostitutes or doormats, either. They just felt happier in themselves and happier as a couple. It didn't mean the other issues in their relationship went away – what it *did* mean was that those issues were discussed and dealt with without sex being a complicating factor. Their men weren't secretly, or not so secretly, nursing a 'lack of sex' grievance that made them resentful, bitter and generally closed to their point of view – whatever the topic.

A lovely German couple wrote to me recently describing their solution to the imbalance of sexual desire in their marriage. They've designated one day a week when they definitely have sex. Wednesday. They plan for it. There is no worrying about when it will happen again, no fear of rejection when they get into bed on a Wednesday. It's a sure thing, so they can concentrate on both of them enjoying it rather than all the other stuff that can and so often does get in the way.

I replied to their initial letter and, after a series of emails, we ended up talking on the phone.

'Doesn't your wife find it a touch unromantic?' I asked. 'I mean, what if she isn't, you know, in the mood?'

'That's the whole point,' the man replied. 'She has to *get herself in the mood*. She knows we'll be having sex at the end of the day, so she has a simple choice: she can either leave it to fate and hope that she just happens to feel like it at nine o'clock, or she can take control and get herself in the mood.'

'How?' I asked, slightly taken aback.

'Well, each person is different, I suppose. Whatever works for you. Gloria lights candles and puts on soft music. Others I know dress in lingerie and read saucy books —'

'You know *others* who do this?' I interrupted.

'Sure,' he replied. 'It's rather taken off as an idea in our town. It's like an open secret among our friends. I reckon we're the happiest married couples in Europe.'

'But isn't it a bit, well . . . clinical?' I persisted. 'A little bit like shooting fish in a barrel?'

'It's a matter of perspective,' he replied. 'We think nothing of being proactive about our fitness, health and finances, yet when it comes to our sex lives we're led to believe it's all just going to happen by magic, without any thought or planning. I call it loading the odds in favour of intimacy and fun. Remember, there's nothing forbidding you to stop if it isn't working for you.'

'Ah, that's a good point,' I said, seeing my chance to get the other side of the story. 'And how many couples try this and then give it up after a few weeks?'

'None.'

'*None?*'

'None that I know of. Why would you? My wife and I have being doing it for eight years now. I wish we'd started earlier.'

'I'm still not convinced,' I replied. 'Part of me just can't help thinking that sex should be unplanned and surprising, and happen when the moment simply grabs you . . .'

'Nigel, I think you're getting it out of perspective. It's about trying to promote physical closeness and general intimacy in a loving relationship. Some people join a bowling club – we just happen to choose to have sex together. Come to think of it, we've joined a bowling club as well, but that's besides the point – or maybe it isn't, actually.'

'What do you mean?'

'Well, part of the beauty of this idea is the add-on benefits,' he explained. 'At first, the only times we had sex was on a Wednesday, then after a while we found we were having sex in an "unplanned" way at other times during the week as well. It's brought us closer together, full stop. I think you're taking this and yourself too seriously, Nigel. It's a shame to see so many marriages die in the bedroom. It's not just teenagers who should have all the fun, you know.'

He was so convincing that I spoke to a number of friends about the German couple and their 'nominated day' approach. Within a week an American friend had given me the other side of the coin.

'I've already tried it, Nigel. It was a disaster.'

'Really? Why?' I asked.

'Well, a few years ago we agreed that Tuesday night would be *the* night. And on one level I have to admit it worked. He'd come home on Tuesdays and we'd have sex. It was fun. Pete, in particular, was in heaven. He was noticeably happier – not just on Tuesdays but throughout the week. It removed a longstanding source of tension in our relationship,' she said.

'If you don't mind me saying, it doesn't really sound like a disaster,' I pointed out.

'No, trust me, it was. I started to notice that the only time he ever showed me any tenderness was on a Tuesday. He'd kiss me before he left for work. Call me from the office and leave me sweet messages. Give me flowers in the evening with a hug. Lovely stuff, but during the rest of the week – nothing. No hand-holding or cuddles. We'd just go about our business as if we were domestic colleagues, not romantic partners.'

She was very bitter about the whole thing and we ended up having a conversation long into the night. For this couple the nominated-day experiment had made their relationship worse, not better. A useful reminder, if it were needed, that one solution hardly ever works for everyone.

I think there is another lesson from her story, however. While she was articulate about describing her needs and dissatisfactions to me a couple of years after the fact, it was clear she hadn't communicated them to her husband at the time. Now, I know he should have behaved differently anyway, but this example goes to the heart of the issue. For a long-term relationship to be joyful both partners should be clear about their needs and both partners should lovingly try to accommodate them. For a man to ignore his wife's clearly expressed desire for more regular and loving tenderness is every bit as bad as a wife choosing to ignore her husband's sexual frustration. It's about caring, empathetic communication. To my mind, the end-game here is not more sex. The end-game is *a better, more loving relationship.*

I might have taken issue with my American friend's communication skills but the nominated day approach didn't work for me either. After these conversations and having carefully considered both the pros and the cons I decided to give the 'fixed day a week strategy' a go in my own life. Now it's never easy to pick the right time to raise something like this, but on this occasion I felt I excelled myself. Rather than raise it in the middle of an 'I want more sex' argument, I chose to bring it up at the end of a particularly delightful and relaxed dinner out.

'Sweetheart, can we fix a day when we regularly have sex?' I hopefully enquired.

'Sure,' Kate replied. 'How about 10 August?'

*

It's important to stress I'm not advocating that women have more sex with their partners just 'for' men. I'm advocating that they have more sex for their partners, their partnership and, crucially, for *themselves*. It shouldn't be simply about making someone *else* feel better. It should also be about making *you* feel better.

It's as if there are four levels to the whole 'sex after kids' thing.

The first level is to simply stop having it. This is not as uncommon as you may think.

The second is to have it irregularly in a way that makes both parties feel bitter, resentful and miserable. Again, this level includes a tragically vast number.

The third level is for the woman to lovingly accommodate her man's needs. To my mind (and remember, I'm speaking as a very short man, not an expert), this is an improvement on levels one and two. But still not the ultimate answer.

The fourth is for a couple to engage in intimacy that provides physical and emotional satisfaction for *both of them*. That doesn't mean multiple shared orgasms every night. It means getting to a stage where if someone said to a couple they could no longer have sex with each other, they would *both miss it*.

This is one area where I don't advocate my previous 'lower your standards' observation. In fact, quite the reverse. I think in many cases to get to level four involves raising your standards and expectations of what you can and should be getting from your sex life. If your goal is simply to shut your husband up, then it's unlikely you're going to go past level three.

I believe to get to level four takes work for all but the lucky ones. Work that may involve you trying stage three for a good while before progressing. Work that will have its disappointments, frustrations and setbacks. But work, all the same, that I passionately believe is worth the effort.

More than worth it, in fact. I feel it provides a sensationally, positively, absolutely gobsmackingly wonderful return on a minimal investment. Remember when you used to look forward to and loved having sex? Well, I don't want to come across like Sting, and call me an old softy if you must, but I believe it is possible for couples to resurrect and maintain that feeling well into their eighties – and beyond. What you do may change, but the benefits and rewards can actually increase with age, not fade.

In the end, it comes down to communication, I suppose. In my business talks, I always advise company leaders to try to over-communicate with their staff (something it is actually impossible to do). This is one of the rare areas where I think family life can learn and benefit from good business practice. All too often, sex is the one thing that is avoided and not spoken about in a marriage, when in reality it is the very subject about which we should make a point of trying to over-communicate if we are to find sexual contentment and joy in a lifelong partnership.

There are far too many books already on the mechanics of what to do in the bedroom and, frankly, I'm the last person to ask. All I would like to observe is that this is one area where the marketing cliché 'less is more' is most definitely not applicable.

If you ask me, 10 August or no 10 August, 'less is less and more is great'.

Packed Lunch

Kate is not a morning person. Every day, I wake her up by bringing her a cup of tea in bed. Call me a limp-wristed romantic but I've been doing it since we were married.

Most days, she says something like 'not now, it's too early' or 'why didn't you wake me earlier, it's too late' or 'have you taken the dog for a walk?' or 'not Earl Grey – I want green tea'. Every time, I think, *something like 'thanks, sweetheart' would be nice*. Still, I keep on doing it. And the reason I keep on doing it is I've come to realise that we are different. And being different is a good thing. As long as you can learn to adapt to each other.

For far too many years, I spent enormous energy trying to change Kate's morning persona. I'm naturally at my most perky and alive in the morning. I wake up and feel incredibly joyful about having been given another day on this planet to fill. A friend once told me you can divide people into two camps – those who wake up and say 'God, another day' and those who wake up and say '*Good*, another day'. It would be fair to say I fall into the latter camp. More often than not, when I wake, I want to leap out of bed and conquer the world. What's worse, I want to *talk* about it. You can imagine how utterly hideous this must be for Kate, who just wants to be left alone to drag herself slowly awake at her own pace.

Time after time, I would bring her a cup of tea after my morning run and start talking at her. And I mean *at* her. I would get increasingly agitated as her response to my plans for global domination were met by a grunt or just silence. Not getting the type of response I wanted from her, I would ramp up the urgency to see if I could ignite the desired energetic and enthusiastic acknowledgement. Of course, it had the opposite effect and she would get even more taciturn. Then snappy. I don't do snappy. I can't let it lie. If you mutter something under your breath like 'took your time' or 'so you left the dishwasher open overnight *again*', I can't help but confront it. Atmosphere and tone drive me up the wall. It makes me hell to live with.

I can escalate a minor snipe from my wife into all-out marital war within thirty seconds. In fact, I frequently did in the mornings until one day a friend of mine – Bill – repeated a phrase to me that he had recently read: 'There's no point shouting at a cat in an attempt to get it to bark.' I don't know why this particular phrase resonated with me, but the penny just seemed to drop. *Leave her alone in the mornings, Nige – just bring her a cup of tea and keep your big mouth shut.*

I tried it, and the effects were immediate and dramatic. I spared Kate my morning's visionary plans. In fact, I didn't talk at all unless she initiated conversation. More revolutionary still, I attempted to let any snappy or sour-toned remarks go 'through to the keeper'.

The first time I did this, I was positively boiling with rage at some ungenerous remark Kate had made in response to my efforts at cooking the kids' breakfast. Not 'thanks, darling' but 'Nigel, I was saving the bread for their packed lunches', said in that mildly withering tone that is generally followed by the unspoken clause 'you stupid fuckwit'. It's not only the tone of voice, either – it's her 'tone of face' that packs a punch as well. I'm told that eighty per cent of communication is non-verbal. Well, in Kate's case, she puts the whole 100 per cent to good use.

This time, however, instead of saying 'why don't you sod off – I was just trying to be helpful, you ungrateful cow', I said nothing. It was hard, but I got out of the house without saying anything defensive, aggressive or sarcastic.

On the way to work, I was running over in my mind the argument I was planning to have with her in the evening when my mobile rang.

'Hello?' I answered.

'Hi, sweetheart – it's me. I'm just calling to say sorry for being such a cow this morning. Eve got me up four times in the night and I'm bollocksed. I really appreciate you getting them ready for school and starting the breakfast. I don't know what I was talking about with the bread – we both know there's an extra loaf in the freezer – sorry. Luv ya,' she said, then hung up.

I almost crashed the car. Instantly, I was no longer angry. In fact, I felt like a prick for even having felt angry in the first place.

Just the simple act of biting my lip had transformed a potentially negative relationship-souring situation into a hugely positive relationship-enhancing one.

I'm a country mile away from being a saint at this, but the simple strategy of trying to adapt to how Kate is rather than *change* how she is has never failed to make the situation better, not worse.

Removing the Plank

My experience of trying to live better with Kate in the mornings has actually changed one of my core life philosophies. Basically, I now attempt to waste no energy in trying to change or 'improve' other people. That doesn't mean I don't try to help if asked, or attempt to bring my kids up right. What I'm talking about is those situations where I decide I want to change something in my life. In the past, I would invariably drag other people into my crusades.

To take a trivial example, if I thought the house was too messy and wanted to do something about it, I would talk to Kate and tell her the house should be tidier and that *we* should do something about it. Fine up to a point,

I suppose. But it would inevitably quickly lead to me criticising her when she failed to be perfect in whatever the new goal was. She would then quite reasonably point out that it wasn't her idea to live in a show home in the first place and that I was far from perfect myself when it came to keeping the place tidy. End result: we would argue and the house would be no tidier.

I've totally changed my approach. Now, if I decide I want to change something, I *start with myself.* If I notice the house is a dump (and it can be with four kids, trust me), I do that most radical of things.

I do something about it.

I, not *we*.

The deal I have with myself is that once I am regularly practising perfection on whatever the current mission is, then and only then can I rope poor old Kate in. Or anyone else, for that matter. Given that you never get to perfection, this never happens. What does tend to happen instead is that your partner, or whoever, notices you changing and willingly decides to join in. End result: a sense of working together, no one feeling ordered around – and the house is tidier. If your partner doesn't join in, so what? You have a tidier house anyway, which is what you wanted in the first place.

*

So often in the past I would hide behind someone else's imperfections rather than look at my own. There's a wonderful phrase from one of the gospels – 'take the plank out of your own eye before you concern yourself about the speck of sawdust in someone else's'. Humans have an extremely strong defence mechanism against taking responsibility for their own lives. It can all so easily become someone else's fault – your partner, the kids, the neighbours, the government, the Americans, society, the company you work for. The list is endless. And can lead to quite astonishing levels of self-delusion.

I've had numerous conversations in the past with overweight people who passionately and genuinely believe their problem is someone else's fault. It would be funny if it weren't so tragic. Hugely overweight, sedentary people trying to persuade me with all their hearts that it is the fault of the food industry or fast-food restaurants, or the government, or their parents. Anyone's but their own. It can become self-fulfilling. If we allow ourselves to think and act like this, we can end up never mixing with anyone who has the guts – or cares enough – to ask whether we'd ever considered that it (whatever 'it' is) is our *own* fault. We find a tribe who collude in group denial.

I used to drink too much because of me. I used to eat too much because of me. I used to have no balance in my life because of me. I couldn't swim because of me. I had an impressively long list of reasons why these things were all someone or something else's fault. Then, one day, a mid-life crisis saved me. I realised I was talking rubbish and that my life was my responsibility. The moment I did, all the above things changed. Permanently.

I had spent decades trying, and failing, to give up drink and lose weight through other people. It never worked. Once I realised that it was me and me alone who needed to take responsibility, I got sober and slim. Same with the swimming and life balance. I'm not saying it is easy. I am saying that there's no substitute for taking a long, hard look at yourself, not at other people.

Back to the house example. The truth is, the house was a mess, both because I wasn't pulling my weight in clearing up after the kids and because personally I set a bad example. I used to chuck my briefcase on the sofa, kick off my shoes and leave them on the kitchen floor, step over my gym kit rather than put it in the wash, etc. Who the hell did I think I was, asking other people to tidy up the house? The problem had nothing to do with Kate. It had everything to do with me. As I said, we can be very, very good at self-delusion. Especially if it gets us off the 'it's up to you' hook.

I'm a huge believer that everyone has vast potential for positive growth in their lives. But the tragedy is that for millions, that potential lies untapped for a lifetime.

It's realising *you* are the one responsible for making whatever changes you want in your life that, to my mind, is one of the essential steps towards unlocking that potential. Even if the problems that you are facing *are* someone else's fault, there is still no alternative to taking personal responsibility for resolving them.

After all, when your car blows a tyre on the motorway, you don't walk back down the road to harangue the nail that did it – you get out the spare and change the wheel.

Not a bad analogy for life in general in this short man's opinion . . .

Nancy Kline

Pausing before I speak, adapting to my audience, being mindful of my impact on others, leaving certain things unsaid, reminding myself to be appropriately supportive and complimentary – all are valuable, and sometimes painful, lessons. But there is one thing above all others that has transformed my communication skills, and relationships, in recent years.

Listening.

I'm not talking about simply letting others get a word in edgeways. I'm talking about proper listening. 'Higher order listening', for want of a better phrase.

It wasn't a lesson that came easily or quickly. Quite frankly, for many years I was a shamefully poor listener.

Then, a few years ago, a friend of mine told me about a woman called Nancy Kline. I read up on her and was astonished and appalled in equal measure. Her theory is quite simple. She believes that listening well is a radical act – one that not only ignites the mind of the person doing it but also *improves the intelligence of those you are listening to.* Bit of a bold statement, I know, and difficult to accept on first exposure, but bear with me while I try to explain.

In the past, if I asked you a question, you'd be lucky if I let you finish your answer. If I did let you finish, I definitely would have started talking the moment you stopped. Kline maintains that if we didn't start talking when the other person had finished their initial answer, after the briefest of pauses they would start talking again – and that's when we learn the really important things. I tried it and, to my astonishment, discovered she's right. What's appalling is that I spent thirty-five years *never getting to those important things.* Whether it was with my wife, friends, family or colleagues at work, I had been unwittingly cutting myself off from a whole world of learning and connection. Kline argues that if you don't say anything once they've finished a second time, they will start talking once more – and this time you'll learn the *really* important stuff. When they stop a third time, if you ask a well-placed question – yep, they'll start again. And again, the quality of what you learn will be even richer.

Now, imagine for a moment you were working or living with me, and I've been listening to you in my old way for a couple of years. Regularly interrupting you and jumping in the moment you finished answering one of my questions. If I ask you a question after two years of this 'listening', the quality of your answer will be directly affected by the type of attention you know I'm going to give it. You'll likely rush to get your point out, as you're afraid I'll interrupt before you finish. You'll try to condense your whole thinking into your first couple of sentences because you know that when you draw breath, I'll seize the floor again and your opportunity to make your point or express your feelings will be gone. Or maybe you'll simply not put too much thought into your answer because you know how fleeting and cursory my attention to it will be. Basically, the types of answers I was limiting myself to receiving for thirty-five years.

Now, imagine an alternative scenario. This time, you've been living or working with me for a couple of years and I have been regularly and consistently listening to you in the way Kline recommends. Never interrupting, always letting you finish, giving space for you to think and start talking again, asking well-placed questions to prompt you to elaborate and clarify. After two years of this type of attention, if I ask you a question, I *guarantee* the quality of your thinking will be higher than in the first scenario. If you know someone is going to listen respectfully and genuinely consider your words, you can't help but give your answer a certain depth of thought.

What's more, this type of listening creates a positive environment in which the way people interact and relate to each other is utterly transformed – at home and in business. I've tried it in both and the effects have been so dramatic that if I wasn't witnessing it in my own marriage and in my own business, I wouldn't have believed it if you told me. If you work in a team and you've never done it before, holding a meeting where you guarantee *in advance* that everyone will be allowed to speak in turn *for as long as they want, without interruption* can literally be a life-changing event. It certainly was for me. I suddenly realised how much I'd been missing.

The German philosopher and theologian Paul Tillich maintained that 'the first duty of love is to listen'. When

I read that in college twenty-five years ago, I had no idea what he was going on about. Marriage, four kids, a career and a mid-life crisis later, I think I finally understand. To love, you have to give *attention* to another person.

I'm by no means perfect at listening – far from it – but I am better. And the benefits of being better are so utterly, fabulously wonderful that at the risk of sounding like a raving fanatic, I want them for everybody. Naive as it may be, I passionately believe that if enough people learnt to listen better, it would transform not just our families, companies and communities – it would transform the world. If you only take one thing from my observations on communication, I plead with you to make it this – get hold of a copy of Nancy Kline's book *Time to Think* and read it from cover to cover.

By all means, send me a rude email if, having done so, you don't think it was worth it.

Marco Polo

A large part of my decision to try to construct a life that doesn't mean I occupy most of my waking hours in an office, or commuting to an office, is my desire to be a meaningful part of my kids' lives. I want to actually spend some time with them. Not the scraps of interaction that many working mums and dads have to make do with, but proper, regular time.

Desiring it and doing it, however, are two different things entirely. Be careful what you wish for, as a wise man once said.

The first school holidays after my step back from the office were, shall we say, a bit of a shock. For the previous three years during every school holidays, I was working *and* we had a nanny. This does tend to shield you from the brutal reality of what living with four young kids for twenty-four hours a day, seven weeks in a row is like.

I love my kids to the ends of the earth, but sometimes they can be so frustrating that I wish they *were* at the ends of this earth. During my previous year off, I had learnt the nuts and bolts of how to deal with them. These days, I could make a packed lunch and put their laundry in the right place quicker than you could say 'new-age metrosexual', but I was yet to develop the skill of being able to cope calmly with their behaviour. I think I have a rare medical condition that makes me physically allergic to whinging and whining. The moaning whimpering of a complaining young child cuts right through me. When all four of mine are doing it at the same time, it makes me want to kill someone – usually myself. As I wash up the dishes after dinner with a thumping headache and a heavy heart at my inability to bring up well-mannered, helpful humans, as opposed to the revolting chimpanzees they can at times resemble, I often find myself losing the will to live.

On top of the whinging and whining, there is the fighting. A friend of mine, Paul, claims his two sons have an all-embracing 'simple, sequential, four-stage daily routine – wake up, start fighting, stop fighting, go to sleep'. Mine aren't quite that focused, but I know where he's coming from. Thing is, my kids have the capacity to test the patience of a saint even when they are happily *playing*. There is a game they play with their friends. It's called Marco Polo and the rules are simple. Very simple. The child who is 'it' closes his or her eyes. They then have to find the other children, with the aid of the 'Marco Polo' call. Every time the child who is 'it' calls out 'Marco!' all the others have to call back 'Polo!', thus temporarily revealing their location. A harmless and amusing way of passing five minutes, you would think. Except they don't play it for five minutes. I've known them to play it for five hours. Trying to work from home while a crowd of kids repeatedly chorus 'Marco . . . Polo' outside your window can make commuting to an office seem a strangely sensible idea.

However, it's not just the general stuff that drives me wild, it is the specific moronic behavioural traits that push me over the edge. I've lost count of the number of times that one of my children has walked into a room where one of his brothers or sisters is quietly sitting watching the TV and, rather than sitting in any of the other sixteen comfortable places in the room that have a clear, uninterrupted view of the television screen, sat *right next* to his sibling. As sure as the polar caps are melting, the little buggers would then start irritating each other and, before long, a previously calm and harmonious room would be the scene of a noisy all-out war.

To be fair, my own behaviour as a kid could be a tad irritating at times. In an attempt to lighten the domestic burden at an early age, Mum and Dad allocated both of us jobs around the house. One of my tasks was washing up the dishes after each family meal. My brother's job was to dry and put away the dishes after me. Now, John is no fool and he quickly worked out that he could simply leave my washing up on the draining board to air-dry before putting it away, thereby allowing him to go and watch TV or play a game instead.

This really pissed me off. Not just that I would be left alone in the kitchen with no one to talk to while washing up. It offended my young sense of justice. Why should he be able to get away with not doing his full job when I had to do mine? I therefore took to a new daily strategy of going into the kitchen secretly every five minutes and pouring a jug of water over the dishes on the draining board. It took a hell of a lot of determination and effort, but every five minutes I would excuse myself from whatever I was doing and go and give those pots and dishes the 'freshly washed, need drying' look. John would return to the kitchen after an hour, sometimes two, to find to his astonishment that the plates and cutlery were still dripping wet. When I was finally rumbled, it would be fair to say my mother's patience ran out rather spectacularly.

There used to be a sign in the girls' kindy that said: 'Patience is finite so can't be relied on to not run out. Understanding, however, is inexhaustible.' In its way, a profound thought and one I'm trying to learn from.

I remember when I took Alex to the local park – Priory Park in North London – for his first bike ride without training wheels. Priory Park has an enormous concrete area for bikes and skateboards. I'd got him up early so we would have this ideal space all to ourselves. Which we did – all bar one young mum pushing a pram in the far distance.

'Off you go, mate – show your dad what you can do. Just make sure you steer well clear of that lady in the distance. Prams and bikes don't mix,' I said.

Alex pushed off and proceeded to ride at high speed across the entire park, straight into the middle of the pram. Knocking himself, the woman and the baby to the ground. There was literally no one else in the park. Just acres of empty space surrounding a pram on its side with Alex's bike sticking out of it.

The actor Peter Ustinov defined love as 'an act of endless forgiveness, a tender look that becomes a habit'. Substitute 'parenting' for 'love' and I reckon they are not bad words of advice for any prospective father. I've come to believe, however, that it is unrealistic and pointless for most of us to naturally and easily understand our children's behaviour. That doesn't mean you should stop trying. Just like you wouldn't sit down at a piano for the first time and expect to be able to play like a maestro, why would we expect to be immediately good at being parents? Parenting is a skill, and just like other skills it takes work, hard work, to acquire it. There are a few who are naturals but for the rest of us it involves practice, endless mistakes, an ability to be flexible and a willingness to learn.

Just maybe a domineering father who points out a pram in the far distance to his inexperienced, scared and excited eight-year-old is making it *more* likely the child will ride into it. I clearly remember driving lessons with my father where I was so overwhelmed to be actually spending one-on-one time with him and desperate to please him that I could never go more than 100 metres without stalling the engine or grinding the gears. Yet put me in a car with my mates and I could drive like I'd been doing it for years.

I spent far too much time thinking the secret to successful childrearing was discipline. Of course discipline is part of it, but far too often it is used as an oversimplistic and convenient panacea to hide behind. Bringing up kids isn't a military operation, or shouldn't be, in my opinion. Just telling a kid what you want her to do in an ever more stern manner may not be the most effective strategy. It's like those tourists who can't speak the language and feel shouting louder is going to make the difference. When Alex was first able to be fed in a highchair I had awful trouble getting him to sit still and stop struggling and wailing to get out of the chair. To my annoyance a firm tone and harsh language had no effect whatsoever. At the end of my tether, I asked the advice of a friend of ours, Terry.

'How do you think I can get Alex to sit happily in his highchair?'

'Grapes,' she replied.

'Grapes?'

Overworked and Underlaid

'Yep, grapes. Get two grapes, cut them in half and, without saying anything, place the four pieces flat side down on the tray in front of him,' Terry explained.

'Is that it?' I dubiously asked.

'Yep – give it a try and let me know how you go.'

To my astonishment, it worked. Alex spent the entire time contently sliding the four halves of grape around his highchair tray while I prepared his food and spoonfed him. I could have spent twelve months trying to 'discipline' him to no effect, yet one simple piece of advice from an experienced mum and I was sorted.

I now try to spend less time clinging to fixed ideas about how to bring up my children. (I've also come to realise that just because a tactic works with one child it doesn't necessarily mean it will work with another.) Instead I'm learning to focus on the outcome I want. This frees me up to learn from other parents who are good at it – either naturally or from bitter experience.

Surprisingly, the single most useful piece of advice I have received in this area came not from a mum who was an expert in dealing with young kids but from an elderly grandfather whose children had left home decades ago. 'Just remember, Nigel,' he said slightly mournfully. 'The days may be long but the years are short. Never forget to enjoy them while you've got them. They'll be gone before you know it.'

The days may be long but the years are short. Not bad words to remember next time you're struggling with a 'Marco Polo moment'.

Philip Larkin

Unfortunately, when my patience runs out, or rather my understanding is found lacking, my language has a tendency to deteriorate rather dramatically. I think I get it from my dad. I'll never forget the family holiday we had in Cornwall. I don't remember it for the great times on the beach or the fun party games. Instead, I remember it for the night when all the lights went out.

The whole family had been sitting at the kitchen table, eating dinner, when it happened. Dad got up to find the fuse box. He felt his way, arms out like a blindfolded person, from the room. The rest of the family sat silent in the dark, waiting hopefully for the lights to go back on and dinner to be resumed. The silence was broken a

couple of minutes later by a loud crash, followed immediately by an even louder roar as Dad angrily shouted,
'Jesus Fucking Christ!! It's as Dark As Satan's Arsehole In
Here!!' It's difficult to describe how powerful an impact
that had on an eight-year-old whose mother *and* father
constantly told him to watch his language. They never
swore in front of my brother and me – unless they stubbed
their toe in a dark and unfamiliar holiday cottage, that is
– yet one of my clearest childhood memories is the 'Satan's
Arsehole incident', as John and I still refer to it.

A dear Aussie friend of mine told me an instructive
story about her own swearing. She is called Cait; her
husband, Andrew. They have three delightful young
kids.

'It was last summer, while my parents were staying,'
Cait said. 'They'd come down to Sydney from Orange
for a week to spend some time with their grandkids. We
were all having lunch together on the first day when
Banjo [their five-year-old son] knocked over his drink at
the lunch table. Nothing unusual there – he does it all
the time. It was what he said that was awful.'

'What did he say?' I asked, intrigued.

'Fuckinandrew,' she replied.

'Fuckinandrew?'

'Yep. "Fuckinandrew." We all pretended we hadn't heard, but then in the car, on the way to the beach, I beeped my horn at someone and Banjo shouted from the back seat, "Fuckinandrew!" On the beach, his sister bit him and he shouted "Fuckinandrew" at her.' Cait shook her head. 'My mum was aghast, so I made a big scene of telling him off in front of her.'

'How did that go?' I asked.

'Disaster. He just looked at me with tears in his eyes and said, "But Mummy, it's what you say all the time."'

Fuckinandrew indeed.

The point, I suppose, is that your children learn not from what you tell them but from what they see you *doing*. I find it a terrifying thought – the gap between my intentions and my behaviour being so cavernous.

My father only hit me once. I was nine. We were playing cards in the evening as a family. It was the night he was going to teach me the rules of bridge so I could finally join in with the grown-ups. When it came to my turn, I laid the queen of spades on the table.

'You can't play that card, mate,' Dad said.

'Yes, I can,' I replied.

'No, as I explained, you have to follow suit. Hearts were led, so you can't put a spade down.'

'Yes, I can.'

'No, you can't. I know you've got two hearts in your hand, so you can't play a spade.'

'Yes, I can.'

'Darling, you can't – it's against the rules,' he implored.

'It may be against the rules, but I can still put it down. I just did,' I said, smugly pointing at the offending card on the table.

Whack. My father lashed out in utter frustration and smacked me on the cheek.

You can see his point – I'd have belted me as well. At least he kept his hand open.

Like my father, as a rule I don't hit my kids. It's been over ten years now and to date I've only broken the rule once. Last year, in fact. I'd had an awful day at work. When I came home, the kids were being more than usually energetic and noisy. Kate was frazzled from a long day with them and asked me to take them to the park. I didn't want to. I just wanted to run away and lie down in a dark room. There was a delicate problem in the office that I was expected to sort out the next day, and I needed some undisturbed thinking time to gather my thoughts and decide on the best course of action. Despite my private reluctance, I could see Kate needed a break, so I agreed to take them to the park.

It took me an age to get them all ready. They squabbled over everything.

Everything.

Eve wanted to wear Grace's shorts, Harry didn't want Alex to borrow his skateboard, none of them wanted to wear a hat. Just as it looked like we were ready, one of them said she wanted to go to the loo. Then all of them did. Having finally got them outside the front door, I checked if they had put on sunscreen, as I had repeatedly asked them to do. None of them apart from Grace had, so we had to go back in the house. They proceeded to fight over who got the sunscreen tube first. Harry pushed his sister. Eve burst into tears. From the kitchen, Kate shouted, 'Make sure you take the dog. She needs a good walk.' Damn, I didn't want to take the dog. They fought over who would hold the dog lead.

Then the phone rang. It was the office – apparently, there was an emergency and they *had* to talk to me. I shouted to Kate, asking her to tell them that I would call them from the park in five minutes. It started to rain. I couldn't face attempting to get the kids to put on their coats, so I ushered them out the door to face the elements in their shorts and T-shirts.

When we got to the park, I had well and truly waved goodbye to the end of my tether. I sat down on a wall and put my face in my hands. I just wanted sixty seconds of peace before I called the office back.

'Dad,' a girl's voice said as a small hand tugged at my shirt.

'Not now, sweetheart. Daddy's having a rest,' I told whichever one of the twins it was.

'Daaad,' the voice implored as the hand tugged again.

'Seriously, just give me a moment, darling. I'll be with you in a minute,' I said, my face still in my hands.

'Daadyyee.' The voice was getting insistent, the tugging more forceful. The throbbing, dull ache behind my left eye was becoming a full-blown migraine.

'If you don't stop pulling at my shirt, Daddy's going to get angry,' I muttered through clenched teeth.

'But Daaaddyyeeee,' the voice said before three really quite violent tugs in quick succession.

'For the love of God, just bloody well leave me alone for one second, would you?' I shouted as I lashed out and smacked Grace on the back of her thigh.

The look of utter trusting incomprehension on her

face is one I've long since given up trying to forget. Her bottom lip started to quiver.

'I picked you a daisy to cheer you up, Daddy,' she said before starting to quietly cry. Sure enough, she was indeed holding a daisy in her hand.

Marvellous. Grace had been the only one of my kids that afternoon who *hadn't* been annoying. Instead, she'd thoughtfully and lovingly gone and picked me a flower to cheer me up.

And I repaid her by hitting her.

At least I'd been acting like a twat when my dad hit me over that card game so many years ago. What life lesson was this going to teach Grace? As I took her in my arms to apologise and comfort her, I noticed to my horror that there was a red mark in the shape of my hand on the back of her leg.

I'm not a big poetry fan, but the opening verse of Philip Larkin's 'This Be the Verse' is just about the most perfect four lines I have ever read:

> They fuck you up, your mum and dad.
> They may not mean to, but they do.
> They fill you with the faults they had
> And add some extra, just for you.

I had a client who told me that at the birth of each of his children, the first thing he did was stand over their cot and apologise profusely for all the mistakes he was undoubtedly going to make in bringing them up. I didn't know what he was talking about at the time, but now it makes awful sense.

I console myself with the thought that the results of our inappropriate role-modelling as parents are not always as dramatic as the card game and daisy incidents suggest. Indeed, on occasions it can be quite sweet.

Once we were visiting our family in England. On this trip, my brother had arranged for Alex and Harry to spend a day at their cousins' school. Jack and Ollie are of a similar age and, like Alex and Harry, go to the local state school round the corner from where they live. Bruton School had been wonderful about it and was keen to host two Australian schoolboys for the afternoon.

That night, I called my brother to ask how it had gone.

'Wonderful – but funny, mate,' he replied.

'What do you mean "funny"?' I asked.

'Well, at the end of the day, the headmistress got the whole school together to say goodbye to Alex and Harry.'

'Sounds lovely,' I said.

'Yeah, it was. Everyone really enjoyed having them, not just Jack and Ollie.'

'Can't see what's funny about it, though.'

'Well, the headmistress gave a little speech about how nice it was to have "our two Australian friends" with us for the day and sent best wishes from Bruton School to Bronte School. She then asked Harry if he wanted to come to the front and say a few words. He declined. So she asked Alex. At first he said no, then thought about it for a bit and said, "Okay, Miss, I'll say a word or two." He then walked to the front of the hall and spoke . . . for *forty-five minutes*. He told the school about how Australian money is waterproof so it doesn't matter if you get it wet at the beach. How Canberra is the capital but not the largest city. He explained the problems the Waratahs are having at fly-half. He went on without pause or notes for three-quarters of an hour.' He laughed. 'Three-quarters of an hour – who on earth taught him to be so ridiculously verbose?' he asked.

'Can't possibly think,' I unconvincingly replied.

Tight Pussy

I am beset with the peculiar affliction of being embarrassed not just by my own blunders but also, rather strangely, other people's as well. In fact, I think it's fair to say I suffer worse if it's someone else's pratfall I am witnessing. It amazes Kate that I have to leave the room if someone on TV is making an unwitting arse of themselves.

'But you don't know them and will never meet them,' she not unreasonably protests.

In my heart, I know she is right, but it doesn't stop the embarrassment being every bit as real.

I suspect this heightened capacity for 'projected embarrassment' might stem from a childhood occasion with my mother that I have long since tried, and failed, to suppress.

I was nine years old at the time and we were staying in the seaside town of Helston, in Cornwall. I love my mum to bits and was sublimely happy as we were spending an extended summer holiday together after a particularly long term away from her at boarding school. Walking down Helston High Street, hand in hand with my mum, I was as content as it is possible for a nine-year-old to be.

My dad, brother and pet cat Wallis were all at home, waiting for us to return with provisions for a picnic lunch that we were going to eat at the beach later in the day. Wallis was a new addition to the family. My parents had got her as a baby kitten at the start of the holiday. She was the first pet we'd had so was rather a big deal in the family's life that summer. I was looking forward to playing with her when we got back.

Helston High Street has the normal quota of shops selling tourist rubbish that you'd expect of any seaside town. As we were strolling up the hill home, Mum suddenly pulled my hand, pointed to the shop window in front of us and exclaimed with a laugh, 'Look, Nigel!'

She was pointing to a T-shirt with a single cartoon image on the front of a drunk kitten slumped in an empty champagne glass. Underneath the image, in huge, bright lettering, was the simple phrase: 'HAPPINESS IS A TIGHT PUSSY'. My bowels contracted as I turned to look at Mum. Far from being embarrassed, she smiled lovingly and, to my utter horror, read the words aloud. 'Ah,' she said. 'It looks like Wallis would look if she was tipsy. How sweet – "Happiness is a tight pussy". We should buy one each for you and your brother.'

I've had a few, shall we say, 'incidents' in my time, but nothing in the thirty-five years since has ever come even remotely close to how awful I felt in that moment. Petrified, I looked my mum in the eye. She smiled down at me. Visions of having to forever wear a T-shirt at family Christmases that publicly proclaimed my love for a snug vagina hurtled through my mind. I swear, I almost fainted with the awfulness of the situation. She took a step towards the shop door and then suddenly and violently jerked to a stop. The penny had clearly dropped. Her voice took on a different, harder, less jolly tone as she said 'not now, we haven't the time' before marching me up the hill.

Thing is, standing there, I just knew I couldn't face telling her there was an alternative, not-so-sweet meaning to the T-shirt's slogan, even if the penny hadn't dropped.

I would have let her buy two of the bloody things – and worn them if need be. Anything but confront the ghastliness of revealing her innocent and loving mistake.

Looking back over my childhood, there are numerous stories I could tell of embarrassing incidents with my parents. I used to think it meant I had embarrassing parents, until I had four children of my own. Having spent the past eleven years as a parent myself, I have come to appreciate a subtle but vital distinction – it's not that *my* parents were embarrassing, it's that *all* parents are embarrassing.

It doesn't matter how much you love your children. It doesn't matter how cool you are. It is just one of nature's immutable laws. Trying to do the right thing is irrelevant in this regard. In fact, it frequently makes things worse. I've long nursed a grievance that my parents never came to watch me turn out for my rugby team throughout my long-playing career as a schoolboy. As I slogged my guts out on the field every week, I would listen to all the other parents cheering and encouraging their kids, and look to the touchline in a vain hope of spotting either my mum or dad. On the one occasion they did turn up, I literally dropped the ball, I was so surprised, thrilled and nervous when I spotted them.

I promised myself I would rectify the situation when it came to my own children. When Alex and Harry started playing rugby, I went to *every* game. And cheered every tackle, pass and kick. I ran up and down the touchline, vocally and passionately encouraging their every move. Until two years ago and a casual remark Harry made before an important game. We were getting into the family car for the drive to the match, which was being held at Nagle Park.

'Dad?' he enquired with a concerned look on his face.

'Yes, mate,' I replied.

'You aren't going to support today, are you?' he asked.

'Er . . . not if you don't want me to, mate,' I said.

'Oh, good – I find it . . . well embarrassing when you do,' he replied before climbing into the car, visibly relieved.

It was like I had been hit in the stomach with a sledgehammer. I was crushed. I wanted to sit on the floor and weep. All this time, the poor mite hadn't been thinking 'oh wonderful, I've got such a supportive and encouraging dad', but 'I wish my bloody dad would shut up, he is embarrassing me in front of my mates'. And I'd been doing it every week *for two years*.

Towards the end of his long life, Gore Vidal remarked, 'Any reflective person is going to realise that he makes a lot of mistakes.' Knowing *in advance* that it is inevitable that you will regularly and hideously embarrass your kids, however hard you try not to, is strangely liberating. It doesn't mean I wander around making tight vagina double entendres in front of my children, but it does mean I cut myself some parental slack on those occasions when they point out my blush-inducing blunders.

Moshpit

Cutting myself some slack is one thing, cutting some for others can prove to be a little harder. I discovered this inability to forgive in, of all places, church.

My mother was staying with us for the holidays and she wanted to go to a service on Christmas Eve. Although I spent my early years going to church at least twice a week and my student days studying theology, I'm no longer a regular churchgoer. In fact, I hadn't been to church since moving to Australia. Instead, I go to Quaker meetings when I can get away on a Sunday and, as anyone who has been to a Quaker meeting will be happy to tell you, this is definitely not 'church'.

As we've got four young kids and as Granny was on a rare visit, I thought it would be nice to find a church, and service, that would be appropriate for all of us to attend. A little bit of research and I found the perfect place – the Anglican church just up the hill from us was doing 'Family Eucharist' at 6:15pm on Christmas Eve.

It was pouring with unseasonable rain come the day, so all seven of us crammed into the car for the short journey to the church. On arrival, I was touched to see how much effort the vicar and his crew had gone to in order to accommodate the children. The younger ones were given costumes from the crib scene to wear, and the running order had been altered to be as child-friendly as possible without turning the service into a Wiggles concert. We sat near the back, as I didn't want the kids to disturb anyone. The church was soon packed.

Although it was radically different from the stiff and formal church services I was used to as a child, this wasn't what challenged my views of acceptable behaviour. It was the children. Or, more accurately, the parents of the children.

As the service began, a young kid ran out from the pew behind us and skipped down the aisle. He got to the front and sat down on the floor by the pulpit. Now,

I'm well aware of what a pain your own kids can be in public, and how irritatingly censorious strangers can be. *It's Christmas*, I thought. *Kids will be kids – just smile and let his parents go and get him without making them feel as though I'm judging them.* I turned and smiled supportively at the kid's mum and dad behind me. The couple smiled back pleasantly. But didn't move. Instead, the dad leant over and whispered something in the ear of the sister of the offending boy. She immediately edged out of the pew and skipped down the aisle. *Ah, how sweet*, I thought, *they've sent her to bring her brother back.* The sister got to her brother – and sat down. And proceeded to play a noisy game with him. *Surely there's been a mistake*, I thought. The service had started and the poor vicar could hardly be heard over the squawking of these two at the front. I resisted the urge to turn around again. *None of your business, Nige, leave it alone – it's Christmas, chill,* I thought.

Then the baby in the pram beside the pew in front of us threw her rattle noisily onto the wooden bench next to her mum. Her mum picked it up and gave it back. The baby did it again. The mum picked it up and *gave it back*. The baby clearly thought this was an excellent game. The mum obviously agreed. This process continued without so much as a 'shush' for a good ten minutes before the baby got bored and thankfully went to sleep. The vicar, manfully striving to continue with the service over the kindy racket, boomed, 'Let us pray.'

This will shut them up and bring some order, I thought. Perhaps the parents were waiting for the serious business to start before controlling their kids. Nope, not a bit of it. *More* children got up and started mucking around in the aisle. I began to wonder if I was in an elaborate 'you've been framed' hoax and that at any moment a camera crew was going to burst out of a side door and yell 'Gotcha!' at me.

I don't like to think of myself as a stuffy old traditionalist or a killjoy – I'm definitely not 'high church', either – but this was taking the piss. Just downright disrespectful.

But the truly mind-boggling thing was that the parents of these children weren't trying and failing to control their kids – they simply weren't trying in the first place. Having little Johnnie and Jemima running screaming up and down the church during the prayers was clearly fine by them. And, to be fair, fine by the rest of the congregation as well, by the looks of it.

It was *me* who was out of step here, I suddenly realised. Everyone else was happy. Who the hell did I think I was to impose my out-of-date and judgemental views of what is appropriate behaviour in a church onto anyone else?

The service continued. So did the children's moshpit in the aisle. I tried to find it cute.

I actually managed to relax by the end, safe in the knowledge that it was only my, and no one else's, religious experience that had been ruined.

'Wasn't that lovely?' I said to Mum as we walked arm in arm to the car afterwards.

'What do you mean "lovely"?' she snapped. 'It was a shameful disgrace. Why on earth didn't those people control their kids?'

Two people's religious experiences ruined, then.

I'm not frowning at other people's parenting abilities here – well, I am, actually, but at least I know I've got no right to – although I do think there is a lesson to be learnt beyond 'haven't church services changed over the last few years?' It's not just church that has changed, it's libraries, schools, town centres, the media – and, more importantly, people. Everything.

It's just that unless you take a break from something, you don't tend to notice the change, as it happens on an incremental basis daily. It's only when circumstances force you to stay away from something for a significant period of time, like my five-year absence from church, that you notice the difference. Like when friends visit us in Australia and exclaim at the size of our kids, whereas Kate and I have barely noticed a change since the last time they visited.

I've come to realise that basically everything is in a permanent state of flux. And, more importantly, I've come to regard this not as a bad thing but simply the inevitable nature of life.

In my traditional office career, I watch senior executives running round with their hair on fire complaining that the industry is changing and that it's nothing like the good old days anymore. I now view that specific industry, business as a whole, and life in general, as constant white water. We are not floating down the big river of life, as I was once told by a well-intentioned teacher – we're hurtling through the rapids. Things aren't worse or more difficult than they used to be – they just are. It was silly of me to expect the church service to be the same as it was in 'my day'. Things move on. Parents get old, companies go broke, previously unimaginable stuff gets invented. I think Bronte is heaven on earth, yet it looks a damn sight different now than it did 100 years ago. Who's to say whether that change is an improvement or a disaster? Better to accept it as it is now and make the best of it, is my observation – and be sure in the knowledge that it will be a damn sight different again (underwater, probably, if we don't sort out global warming sharpish) in another 100 years time.

I now train myself to expect life to be raging white water, not a meandering stream, and consequently I'm less disappointed when I'm proved right. That's not to say, however, that I wouldn't appreciate being contacted if anyone out there knows of a more appropriate old-style church service I can take my mum and her grandkids to next Christmas . . .

Epicurus

How do you know when you're getting old? It's slightly tragic, all the redefining that my generation does – fifty is the new thirty, and all that. No, actually fifty is fifty. And sixty is sixty. And do you know what? To a genuinely young person, any of those numbers are unimaginably ancient. This truth was brought home to me last year when, at the age of forty-two, I was asked to sponsor a colleague in a 100-kilometre charity walk. He was a young chap who worked in our finance department. As I was the CEO of the firm at the time, I thought it was important to show support over and beyond what I would normally do for the cause in question, so I pledged a not inconsiderable sum if he finished. Two months later, having indeed completed the arduous course (it's an all-day-and-night affair across rough terrain), he again came into my office.

'Hi, Nigel, sorry to disturb you. I'm starting to collect for the Oxfam charity walk we did on the weekend,' he said. 'We finished in record time,' he added proudly.

'I heard – it's a massive achievement, Andrew. Well done for doing it and well done for raising the money. At the risk of being soppy, I think it's an incredibly noble thing for you to have done,' I said while reaching for my wallet.

'You don't need to pay now. I'm just warning people that the money is due soon. For larger sums, a cheque is fine,' he replied.

'No, no, I've got it here,' I said, handing over some notes.

'Excellent, many thanks.' He shook my hand and turned to leave. As he got to the door, however, he stopped. He had a thoughtful look on his face, as if he was about to say something important.

'It's a funny thing, Nigel, but in this process the most generous people have been the old people. Thank you for being so supportive,' he said before walking off to rustle up the rest of his sponsorship money.

The old people. He wasn't trying to be funny or a smartarse. He was trying to be nice. It didn't enter his head that I would take issue or offence at him defining me as old. Why would I? I was clearly in my dotage.

Give me a break – I'm only forty-two, I thought at the time. But I realise now that that little ego-saving word 'only' was purely from my perspective. From his perspective, as a twenty-one-year-old young buck starting out in the world, I was twice his age, a father of four and the oldest person in the office. A prehistoric greybeard.

Another more recent event made me realise that maybe he had a point and that I was getting, if not old, at least older. I was listening to my dentist give me some bad news about my 'retreating gums and bone loss'.

'Doesn't sound good. What can we do about that, then?' I asked.

'Nothing,' she replied.

'Nothing?' I queried.

'Nothing. We'll just have to manage the deterioration.'

It was a real shock, the first time in my life a physical problem had been regarded not as fixable but instead as untreatable wear and tear. I suddenly felt like the green sofa Kate and I had owned since our engagement. We loved it but both knew deep down that it wasn't going to last forever and accepted it was gradually going to fall to pieces in front of our eyes, however many stitches and patches we put on it. We'd agreed to keep using it until it literally fell apart. A strategy I suppose I was going to have to learn to employ with my ailing body.

However sobering the sponsorship and dentist incidents were, I happen to believe that it is a good, not a bad, thing to confront your age honestly and openly. We'd all be a damn sight better off if we learnt to accept things as they are, rather than spend all our energy trying to trick ourselves into believing that the facts of the matter are somehow untrue or misleading. To my mind, this is never more so than in the case of death. The depths of self-deception I sink to in an attempt to kid myself about my age are positively insignificant compared with the gargantuan artifice I construct around my mortality. I can't speak for anyone else, but I never used to muse on the fact that I've only a limited time here on this earth. When the death topic was unavoidable, whatever I might have *said*, I could never quite rid myself of the latent suspicion that although everyone else was eventually going to die, I somehow was an exception and would cheat the grim reaper forever. I know it's preposterous when thought through logically, but nevertheless my default subconscious hardwiring was resolutely set to 'denial'. I imagine I'm not alone. Brooding on your own inevitable demise is hardly healthy.

Or is it?

There is actually a considerable weight of opinion that being mindful of your own death is extremely beneficial. The Quakers' central text is a thing called Advices and Queries. Early on, it contains the question: 'Be honest with yourself. What unpalatable truths might you be evading?' Later, it gets more specific: 'Are you able to contemplate your death and the death of those closest to you? Accepting the fact of death, we are freed to live more fully.'

Initially, I was horrified by this suggestion. I hate the thought that any of my children or Kate are ever going to pass away. And as for me, well, I've already told you I'm the exception that proves the rule about mortality.

Yet the more I think of it – and as more of my friends and family pass away – the more I've come to believe I've got the wrong attitude. Rather than denying death, I now try to embrace it. Not embrace as in welcome, but embrace as in use its reality to force myself to get the most out of my life. I forget who said it but there is a wonderful quote, 'Death is like the dark backing of a mirror that enables you to see', which sums up my new attitude. It's not a bad exercise to consider what you'd like people to say about you at your funeral (because, remember, you *are* eventually going to have a funeral). This can be a pretty sobering process if you are living your life in a manner that makes it even remotely likely they will say any of those things that you would like them to. It certainly woke me up. The cliché that life isn't a dress rehearsal contains a profound and powerful truth.

Of course, what you believe happens *after* you die has a vital bearing on how you view and 'use' death. I've always wanted, and failed, to have some faith in God or an afterlife. Both would have been nice, but try as I might, I just can't buy it. In the past, this belief that after I cark it I simply am extinguished and become nothing more than worm food has made it all the more difficult for me to contemplate my death. However, I recently came across a passage from a bloke called Epicurus (now, he really *is* old) that challenged my thinking. 'Become accustomed to the belief that death is nothing to us,' he advised more than 2000 years ago. 'For all good and evil consists in sensation, but death is deprivation of sensation. And therefore a right understanding that death is nothing to us makes the mortality of life enjoyable, not because it adds to it an infinite span of time, but because it takes away the craving for immortality. For there is nothing terrible in life for the man who has truly comprehended that there is nothing terrible in not living.'

Maybe old codgers have their uses, after all.

Mr Marsh

The fact of death is one thing. The *process of dying* is another altogether.

In 2003, my father became so ill that we had to put him in a home. When I first visited him there, it was deeply distressing. Not because of the standard of care he was getting – that is excellent and loving. What was distressing was his quality of life. This once vital and intelligent man was reduced to sitting hunched and silent in an armchair all day, confused and unable to perform even the most basic of functions by himself. It was heart-wrenching for all who knew him before he was ill – especially my darling mum, who'd spent more than forty years as his wife, travelling the world with him and supporting him unquestioningly in his career, patiently waiting for the day when they could enjoy retirement and a long old age together. If the situation was difficult for us, though, it hardly bore thinking about how bad it was for Dad. His first attempt to take his own life merely confirmed what we all knew. This was not how he wanted to spend his last days. In itself, not an unusual story, I'm sure. I realise that there are far, far worse cases of painful, humiliating and joylessly slow deaths.

The reason I mention this visit in 2003 is not because of the exceptional nature of the circumstances, but because of the visit I have just made – in 2007. Nothing has changed. He is still in that chair. Still doing nothing. Still confused and unhappy and depressed. He has been like that for four years now. Leave aside the devastating effect it has had on my mum for a moment. The question I'd like to ask is, is this really the best way to cope with this situation and situations like it? It's not as if society as a whole isn't going to have to face this issue in increasingly large numbers as medical advances continue to extend our life span. We seem more comfortable burying our heads in the sand than facing the core underlying issue. It's like the elephant in the room that everyone can see but no one acknowledges. What I'm talking about has a horrible name, but there's no other for it – euthanasia. The official definition is slightly less distasteful – the Chambers dictionary my father gave me thirty years ago defines it as 'the act of putting painlessly to death, esp. in cases of incurable suffering'.

Distasteful word or not, it's such a hideously complex and sensitive topic that we seem never to discuss it in polite society. If we do, we're terrified of appearing callous or unloving. It is so very, very difficult to talk about – even more so to write about. I realise I am far too emotional about my dad to be balanced and reasonable. I'm angry. I don't know who with, I'm just angry. Generally and uselessly furious.

Whenever I do get into a rare conversation about it, I always seem to come across one of those self-righteous pricks who lecture me about the 'sanctity of life'. I spent three years at university studying the sanctity of life and don't need another lecture on it, thank you very much. I'm talking about real, raw life here, not arid theological theory. As one of my father's old navy friends said to me through his tears, having just visited my dad, 'You wouldn't keep a dog like that, Nigel.' And he's right. When our pets get distressingly frail and unable to enjoy any quality of life, we put them down. Is that more respectful of their lives or less? I don't know, but it's worth thinking about.

I've come to believe that we all have a duty to design our own lives. I've a suspicion that part and parcel of that duty should maybe involve the right and responsibility to design our own deaths. However unpalatable that notion may have become in modern civilisation, it's not a new idea. Way back at the start of the first millennium, the philosopher Pliny wrote, 'Is not the power of dying when you please the best thing that God has given to man amid all the sufferings of life?' Maybe he had a point. And then . . . and then I'll visit my dad and sit with him for an hour, me babbling on in tears, him in total silence, utterly unresponsive, dribbling and hunched, and just before I leave I'll catch a glint in his eye and be sent into a spiral of self-loathing and despair. Maybe he is in there. Maybe it is a life worth perpetuating for as long as medically possible. Maybe, despite what seem to me to be his clear indications to the contrary, he *does* want to live like that for another month, year or decade.

Clearly, someone cleverer and more emotionally detached than I should be in charge of these things. We are kidding ourselves, however, if we don't face up to the fact that the problem is going to get worse, much worse, in our lifetime, and shoving a whole generation of crusties into old people's homes for decades ain't the answer. If, when I get to eighty-seven years of age, you tell me you can keep me alive because of medical advances until ninety-one, but my quality of life would be the same as the one my dad is now enduring, I'd ask you not to put yourself out on my account. At the very least, I'd like a say in the matter. 'Four more years, boys?' as George Gregan said to the broken and beaten All Blacks in the 2003 Rugby World Cup semi-final – not for me, thanks.

I love my dad too much and could never do it. *He'd* have to do it – and the time for that has long passed, so he's stuck. When I try to take the emotion out of it and look fairly at both sides of the issue, I rather wetly end up intellectually sitting on the fence – it's just that if you look closely, you'll see both my legs are dangling over one particular side.

What Did i Do All That For?

One of the unexpected but pleasant upsides of my decision to step back from my office career and concentrate on other areas is the invitations I receive to events I'd normally never have the opportunity to attend. One such event was a happiness conference held in the centre of Sydney last year. The format was simple: five eminent speakers – and me – were to take turns talking on the topic before inviting questions from the floor and an open debate. I felt ever so slightly out of place. The other speakers were all famous and widely regarded as credible experts, a breed I'm more than a little wary of.

As the evening started, I felt sure it wouldn't be too long before someone would call me a fucker, or some such. There was a decent crowd and the opening speeches were well received. I was billed to speak last. When I finally got to my feet after five speeches on happiness, it didn't seem like there was much to add to the debate beyond an honest point of view.

'Good evening. I've a confession to make – well, three, really. First, I don't believe the *purpose* of human life is to be happy. Second, I don't believe anyone has the *right* to be happy. Third, I feel it is unarguable that throughout history the vast majority of human beings have spent the vast majority of their lives *being* unhappy.'

The MC turned to me with a strange look on her face. A look that said '*this is a* happiness *conference, you muppet*'.

I ploughed on regardless.

'I look around me and see a spoilt generation that has never been conscripted to fight in a war, never had to send its children to bed hungry and that believes it's perfectly acceptable to feel mortally aggrieved that the government hasn't yet managed to organise the universe in such a way that they permanently "feel good". If feeling good was the point of life, then being drunk would be the supreme state of existence. I believe this conference, and indeed society in general, is asking the wrong question. We shouldn't be asking, "How can I be happy?" We should instead be asking, "How can I contribute?"'

Clearly, I've still got a bit of work to do on my speaking career. I did promise, however, that I would stop pretending, and the above is what I believe.

When I took my head out of my arse after my mid-life crisis and started to concentrate less on myself and more on the broader picture, I found that I actually became happier. The less I focused on it, the more I got of it.

I'm not saying we should give everything away and go and work in a leper colony (though that is a particularly worthy and noble existence for the few among us who are saintly enough to do it). I'm simply suggesting that if we looked at our lives as a whole and asked ourselves how we could make 'the world slightly better', as opposed to 'ourselves slightly happier', then the inevitable result would be greater happiness all round.

It's not just that we are asking the wrong *question* – I believe society is looking in the wrong *place*. We tend to look on the outside – at the external things. *If only I could pay off the mortgage, get a bigger car, win the lottery . . . then*

I'd be happier. We also tend to look to the future. *I'll be happy* when *this happens or* when *that happens.* I thought this way myself for many years.

But as I said, I've come to believe this is entirely the wrong way round. It's the battle inside that matters. And it matters now, not in the future. My friend Todd once said to me, 'You know, your problem, Nige, is that you've always got one foot in the past and one foot in the future, which means you're forever pissing on the present.' He had a point.

Owing to a variety of circumstances, I've met and mixed with a number of the rich and famous over the past few years. Without exception, they are no happier than me. And I'm averagely morose. They are richer than me, but they are not happier. In fact, in some cases they are considerably miserable. I'm not saying I wouldn't like their money. I'm not saying it is somehow good or easy to be poor. I'm just saying, beyond a certain basic level, money is not the defining factor when it comes to serenity, happiness and contentment.

There is a wonderful Buddhist phrase: 'Before enlightenment, chop wood, carry water. After enlightenment, chop wood, carry water.' It doesn't matter how much you have, you're still going to have to deal with the real world and all its frustrations and disappointments. More importantly, you are still going to have to deal with that little voice inside yourself. There is no escape from the person in the mirror. You can dull the pain with drugs or alcohol. You can divert your attention from the important stuff with rabid consumption and competitiveness. But at the end of the day, the person looking back at you from the mirror *knows*.

To repeat Jesse Owens' wonderful words, 'The only victory that counts is the one over yourself.' You know if your life is inherently pointless and self-centred. Just as external achievements only very temporarily satisfy the self-esteem monster, riches and belongings only fleetingly fill the void. Time and time again, I've witnessed extremely driven men and women reach the heights of their profession and the heights of personal riches only for them to immediately reset the bar in terms of what they need to achieve and what they need to possess. It's as if they are terrified of pausing and asking the bigger questions. They've gone way beyond providing for themselves and their families. They have more than they'll ever need. Rather than stopping to reassess, they simply redefine what is 'necessary' in their lives. This process goes on until death. I've no doubt it would have for me if not for my wake-up call.

I had a recent business dinner with one such person, who spent the entire meal telling me how big his boat was, how large his house was and how much money he was expecting to earn from his business next year. The boat was indeed extremely big, the house enormously large and the cheque from his business promised to be positively gargantuan. Yet I couldn't help looking over the dinner table at him and thinking, *you are grossly overweight and tragically lonely*. He had millions more than me, but nothing on this earth would convince me to swap places with him. The evening reminded me rather too powerfully of the wonderful question: 'What does it profit a man if he gains the whole world and loses his own soul?'

I'm not saying that I'm better than this man. I'm not. Just that I actually wanted to give him a hug as he sat there boffing on about how rich and clever he was. Of course, I didn't, as men don't do that stuff. Far easier to keep up the bullshit pretence. But in retrospect, I wish I had said something. Amiably signalled that I was interested in a different topic to the 'big boat' stuff; gently pushing the conversation to a less superficial and posturing level. Perhaps if we all spoke up in these situations, we could alter the seemingly relentless dominance of commercial success as the way of keeping score in today's developed societies. It's as if the *only* way of keeping score is dollar value. If something's free, it can't be worth anything. If a hedge fund manager earns $9 million a month and a nurse earns $35,000 a year then it must follow that the hedge fund manager is *worth* more than the nurse. But there *have* to be other measures of value beyond money. Money is an amazingly effective and useful way of judging worth, but it is not perfect. On its own, it's bloody useless.

Is my love for my children worthless because it's got no commercial payback? Is the kids' football coach's time worthless because she doesn't get a return on her investment? Market forces left to their own devices have no moral anchor. Society is going to hell in a handbasket if we insist on treating people as economic units of value rather than human souls.

Patch Adams, the famous and extraordinary clown doctor, remarked in a recent interview, 'There is a soul rot around the world.' I think he is right. But we needn't stick with that choice – we are free to change.

Death can have a beneficial role, if used properly, to stem the relentless tide of shallow one-dimensional thinking. The clichéd questions 'what do you think people will say at your funeral?' and 'what would you like them to say at your funeral?' are not a bad place to start. Would you like people to say 'she was a self-centred tosser who had no one to love, left no useful legacy and was an appalling role model for all the wrong values who unthinkingly burnt up vast amounts of the earth's precious resources . . . but she made enormous amounts of money and got to the top of her profession'? I have met more than a few who live out their lives, wittingly or unwittingly, as if their express purpose is to get that response.

Wal King, the CEO of Leighton Holdings, Australia's largest construction company, put it beautifully when he remarked, 'You don't want to get to seventy-five and say, "Well, shit, what did I do all that for?"'

A Melbourne taxi driver once asked me, 'Mate, if you were told you only had twelve months left to live, would you be doing what you are doing now?'

What a brilliant question.

He was a seventy-year-old immigrant from Eastern Europe and after this bizarre but thought-provoking opening we struck up a long conversation. He was an appalling driver but quite the philosopher. Having established what I did (I was in work at the time), he gently remarked, 'I've never been an MD or well-off, but I'm not a failure. Well, not in my mind, anyway – which is the most important thing. Being a good dad is what counts.'

It didn't come across as a put-down or a self-justifying pose – it just came across as *true*. The meeting I was travelling to went well but in all honesty I feel I learnt more from the taxi ride than the boardroom discussion that day.

My humble observation is that if we shifted our focus from the future to the present, and from the external to the internal, then we might just revolutionise the overall sum of happiness far more effectively and democratically than by hoping 'more money and success in the future' will somehow fix things.

Doesn't stop me entering the lottery, however.

Dropping Pebbles

I have an alternative proposal to modern society's 'get rich' lodestar.

It's equally simple, but less fashionable.

'Do some good.'

I'm not talking about being a 'do-gooder'. I mean being mindful about the impact you have on the world and striving to make that impact a beneficial one – not a negative or neutral one. Leaving the world ever so slightly better than you found it, so to speak.

Now I realise that you're not allowed to say 'do good' for fear of being revealed as personally imperfect.

Well, I'll spare you any pretence, that is what I am – hideously imperfect.

You're also not allowed to say 'do good' for fear of being accused of being judgemental.

Well, maybe, just maybe, there *should* be a bit more judgement in today's world. Not religious or governmental judgement, but self-judgement.

So from the perspective of imperfection and at the risk of being mistaken as a do-gooder and a moraliser, I'd like to make the observation that I see many, many well-off people who in my opinion live a life of breathtaking myopic selfishness.

And yes, I think that it is wrong.

When I was in America recently, I read a front-page newspaper article describing how an investment banker had just set a record by paying $103 million for a residential property in the Hamptons. And get this – that price didn't even include the cost of the house he wants to build on it. On one level, this is funny. On another, it is revolting. And no, I don't buy the ridiculous 'trickle down' defence of such mindless opulence. The fact that the bloke with the $103 million house will undoubtedly employ a couple of gardeners – or whatever – isn't a slam-dunk justification in my mind.

Let's be clear – I believe people have every *right* to live a selfish life.

My suggestion is not that we should pass new laws or regulations, nor should we demonise them, patronise them or try to make them feel bad. Or indeed that we become censorious and blind to our own faults.

My observation is simply that society needs a new vision regarding what it means to be a success.

A concise, compelling and inspirational vision.

I've said before that I feel we are given the wrong role models to aspire to and learn from. Why do we hold up business leaders who have made a lot of money but are twice divorced and live a lifestyle of gross overindulgence as anything to admire? Commercially successful though Jack Welch might be, I feel there are a whole bunch of more suitable people who can teach me how to be a better *man*. I don't need the books either, thank you very much, Jack. Why do we hold up fashion models and film stars as people to admire? There's a world of difference between having a leading role in a film and having a leading role in life. It's not fair or clever to treat them as one and the same.

There seems to be this big fog of confusion. Society has mistaken being beautiful for being good, being famous for being admirable, being rich for being important. Way back in the eighteenth century, British playwright Sir Richard Steele memorably remarked, 'We may learn the little value of fortune by the persons on whom heaven is pleased to bestow it.'

Ever since the secularisation of developed societies, there has been an increasing moral vacuum. Just how widespread and deep-rooted this secularisation is was brought home to me on a recent trip to New York, when I was browsing a stall set up outside a church on the edge of Central Park. The stall was selling a variety of religious trinkets and doing a brisk trade to a group of English teenagers who were buying souvenirs before flying home. A pretty brunette – say, seventeen or eighteen – pointed to the necklaces hanging at the back of the stall and said, 'I'd like one of those silver crosses, please.'

'This one?' the trader replied, picking up one of the crucifixes.

'No, not that one. I'd like one with a little man on, please,' she said.

I suddenly felt very, very old.

In this new age, our leaders have been unable to articulate a sense of great purpose. And this matters. Leadership matters. 'Where there is no vision, the people perish,' as it says in the Book of Proverbs. People used to know what the point was. Now there's no higher authority, we are free to choose the rules – and we've gone and chosen a value system that puts money and power above compassion and generosity. It's as if we don't know what to do with our freedom. But we needn't stick with this.

My observation is we have to change if the human species is to have any hope of surviving past the next few generations. The path we're on isn't just diminishing the human spirit – it's leading to the very destruction of the planet itself. 'Who gives a fuck about the pollution we're causing as long as we're making shitloads of profit' is proving to be a globally self-liquidating philosophy.

However, I also observe, and unshakably believe, that people – all people – are inherently and fundamentally good. But we need a new, compelling vision to leverage that goodness. I'm sorry to inform certain high-profile commentators, but 'enhancing shareholder value' or 'double-digit growth' isn't good enough as a societal rallying cry. Not even close. It's worse than irrelevant, in fact. Why increase shareholder value? Why grow? For what purpose? There needs to be a nobler goal. Once you choose a new vision, everything else changes in quick succession. You change who your role models are, you change how you define success, you change what you *do*.

So what new vision am I proposing? I'm not. I'm just observing that the old one has to go. For my purposes in this book, 'do some good' is a sufficiently broad and flexible new one. Someone far cleverer than I needs to craft something memorable and moving that speaks to the human heart.

I'm not saying never strive to better your circumstances or have fun or get rich. I believe you can do good and get rich. In many circumstances, I believe you can do good *by* getting rich. An American friend of mine once remarked, 'Nigel, there's only one horse in the race. And that horse is called Self-Interest.' I don't believe him personally, but even if he's correct I think it is possible to connect the notion of right and private interest.

I am not talking about trying to be perfect.

Nor am I saying that there aren't millions of people out there already doing good. There are.

I'm saying we haven't got a compelling 'do good' vision that has become society's accepted raison d'être – for everyone.

'Do some good' isn't a cry against self-advancement, self-interest, luxury or 'winning'. It's a criterion by which to judge your life. Are you doing some good? Is there *any* way in which you are making this world a better place? If the answer is no, *that isn't good enough.* Under the 'get rich' value system, the question asked (subconsciously or consciously) is 'am I getting richer?' It is frighteningly possible to be a success under this system and not only never do any good, but do considerable harm.

I'm not talking about kicking it all in and going to live in a cave. In fact, I mean precisely the reverse. I'm talking about still chopping wood and carrying water – but with a new purpose. To do some small iota of good that will help make the world a better place. In short, to serve humanity.

If we all acted just one per cent more lovingly, we would change the world unrecognisably overnight. And you could still have a nice car and a foreign holiday.

I'm talking about small, permanent, liveable-with changes. Refusing to take offence and thereby avoiding a family rift; a helpful word of advice to the office junior; picking up someone else's litter. The small stuff *does* matter. I can either think that my smiling at the bank teller is irrelevant fluffy bollocks, or I can think it is making the world a better place. I choose the latter. If I smile at her, maybe she'll smile at someone else. Maybe if I change my showerhead to a more environmentally friendly one, it *is* saving the planet rather than merely saving a gallon of water.

I can't stop the war in Iraq, but I can be nicer to my neighbour. In fact, being nicer to my neighbour just may help, in some indefinable way, to stop the war in Iraq. I believe each and every act of kindness is like a pebble dropped in a huge lake – it sends ripples out around the world and has positive effects, most of which we never get to see. Or understand. The more pebbles we drop, the more ripples there are.

I've a sense that there is actually some indefinable spiritual dimension to this. I think of it as if there are two huge universal buckets – one marked 'Good', the other marked not 'Evil', but 'Indifference'. We have a duty to do what we can to keep the 'Good' bucket fuller than the other. You needn't understand the connection – I certainly don't – but it is possible to teach yourself to believe that every small act of good adds to the spiritual wellbeing of mankind or, if you will, flows into the one same 'goodness bucket'. It follows that if everyone contributes one single drop, the bucket will be considerably fuller.

Tolstoy maintained that 'it's not the Napoleons of this world that change history, it's the small people you've never heard of'. Despite the fact that he used the word 'small', not 'short', I find this notion utterly wonderful – it could be *your* drop that matters, that tips the balance over indifference. Not to try to add a drop here and there is to give up. Which strikes me, to put it mildly, as a shame. Martin Luther King, Jr put it far better than I ever could when he remarked, 'We are caught in an inescapable network of mutuality, tied in a single garment of destiny. What affects one directly, affects all indirectly.'

But what if this is all mumbo-jumbo bullshit? What if there isn't a connection between the small and the universal? Do it anyway, I say. The worst that will happen is you'll get to know your neighbour, the bank teller will have a nicer morning, and you'll use less water in the shower. Besides, as Robert Louis Stevenson said, 'To travel hopefully is a better thing than to arrive. The true success is to labour.'

Bricks and Water

I've spent thirty-odd years trying to find a church I could be comfortable in. It's not the buildings themselves that I have a problem with – on the contrary, I love churches. Indeed, both Chartres and Salisbury cathedrals would make it into my top ten places in the world. No, it's what goes on in the churches that makes me uneasy. Each to their own, I say. I'm delighted, jealous even, that other people find the services moving, profound, comforting, rewarding and spiritually nourishing. My personal experience of them, however, is that they always make me feel like a fraud. It's the same no matter what denomination I attend. I just can't stop thinking about the fact that I don't *believe* what is being said. However much I try,

I can't rid myself of the feeling, deep in my heart, that it's all fairytales. Fairytales that I'd love to be able to believe but, with the best will in the world, I just can't.

One of the promises I made to myself after my mid-life crisis was to stop pretending I believed things that I didn't. In all areas of my life, not just in my career. I can't bring myself to pretend to believe a creed so I can be a part of the other nice bits that I find attractive about the religion – sense of purpose, feeling of belonging, all people are equal, love thy neighbour and the like.

Hence my sporadic attendance at the Quaker meeting house, where you haven't got to pretend to believe anything. I'd all but given up hope of ever finding a church I could call my own when I read a quote from an early Quaker, William Penn. 'True godliness,' he said, 'does not turn men out of the world, but enables them to live better in it and excites their endeavours to mend it.' Apart from the fact that it is a beautiful declaration, it got me thinking. Perhaps if I couldn't find a church that suited me, I should build my own. Not physically construct one by hand, but use my inner experience to transform an existing space into a special location that had spiritual significance for me. Not a special location that was separate from my day-to-day life, but a place that was central to it.

It is not the type of thing men usually talk about, so I kept my thoughts to myself. But, secret or not, I couldn't let go of the notion. Perhaps I could have a place that was special and inspiring and nourishing and calming and rewarding (all those things I wished church could be). But just maybe I had been looking in the wrong places. I had been ignoring all the areas I inhabited – house, beach, garden, office, park – and was comfortable in and instead limiting myself to places I rarely visited and was ill at ease in. Hardly a recipe for success, when I thought about it.

I had been vaguely musing like this for a couple of weeks when an incident brought some unexpected clarity to my thinking.

I was at the Bronte Beach pool on a Saturday morning with Kate and the kids. We go every week to take part in the swim club events that happen there throughout the year. It's a gorgeous tradition. Everyone is incredibly friendly and welcoming. No one puts on any airs or graces. Work is rarely, if ever, mentioned. It's truly an ego-free zone. All the races are handicapped, so even the most hopeless swimmer like myself has an outside chance of winning at least one race in a season. There are always three or four different events you can take part in and we tend to enter all of them, including the medley – regardless of the fact that it involves four strokes, three of which I can't do. Each race is enthusiastically cheered, no matter who is taking part. It's basically a joyous weekly carnival made up of thirty per cent cheering, thirty per cent laughing, thirty per cent chatting – and ten per cent exercise. The coffee's not bad, either. Without a shadow of a doubt, the happiest, most looked forward to part of my week.

On this particular occasion, I was leaning on the railing, watching my elder son, Alex, racing in the 'seven-lapper freestyle'. By the third lap, Alex was sharing the lead with the swimmer in the lane next to him. By the fifth lap, they were still neck and neck, and a good half a length in front of the rest. Alex is only eleven and it looked as if he was beginning to tire. His co-leader looked strong turning into the sixth lap, but he was at the other end of the age spectrum – sixty-five if he was a day – so I thought there was every chance he, too, might begin to fade soon. His name was Brian – one of the small group of selfless locals who, unpaid and unthanked, help run the swim club. The spectators were yelling their heads off at such a close race.

As they both turned into the seventh and final lap, Alex was behind by a metre. And then, slowly, he began to claw back to an equal footing. Half a lap to go and they were dead level. Everyone was screaming their head off. The result didn't really matter, but I would have been so thrilled for Alex to win as he was new to the club and sometimes lacks a bit of confidence. Coming from dreary, rainy old England, he didn't have the years of swimming practice that most of his Aussie mates did. To win a race against six others in front of a screaming crowd would be just the tonic he needed. I couldn't help myself and leant over the railings, bawling my head off for him to give it everything he had for the last few strokes. He appeared to respond, as three strokes to go and he was an inch in front . . . two strokes to go, three inches . . . last stroke and he'd won by half a foot.

Alex was exhausted. Brian leant over from the next lane, ruffled Alex's hair and lifted his hand in a 'he's the champion' gesture. The spectators were calling out all sorts of encouragement and congratulations. Alex was beaming so hard I worried his face would crack. To my horror, I realised I was welling up. To hide the tears, I turned towards the cliff and pretended to dry my hair with a huge beach towel. My shoulders were actually shaking. *Oh, cut it out, you mincing metrosexual*, I said to myself as I tried to stop my tears. Kate came over from the other side of the pool, where she had been watching the race.

'Did you see that?' she said.

'Amazing . . . wonderful. I'm so happy for him,' I replied.

'No, not the result. What Brian did.'

'No. What are you talking about?' I asked.

'He slowed down in the last lap so Alex could win,' she said.

Come to think of it, it had been a bit strange the way Alex had come back to win after looking so knackered with three laps to go. I hadn't noticed Brian slowing down, but looking at him now I could see he wasn't out of breath.

I waited until he was standing alone before approaching him.

'Brian, that was an amazing thing you did just then,' I told him.

'What do you mean?' he replied.

'Slowing down so my lad could win.'

'Oh.' He looked worried. 'No one was supposed to notice.'

'It will mean so much to him. Thank you,' I said.

'You don't think he noticed, do you?' he asked anxiously.

'Of course not, he was swimming,' I replied.

'No one was supposed to notice,' he repeated.

'It's fine, Brian, honestly. I didn't even notice. It's only my wife who's got X-ray cynical specs,' I assured him.

'Oh, good. Great lad, that boy of yours. Hope he keeps coming,' he said before wandering off to the shower block.

It was then that it hit me. If church is about a sense of community, loving kindness, equality, reminding yourself of the important things in life and striving to be a better person – and if Penn was right and true godliness is about being *in* the world, not turning away from it – then this was my church. Right here on my doorstep. In its own way, it was every bit as beautiful as Chartres or Salisbury cathedral, cut as it was into the cliff with a stunning view of the shoreline round to Tamarama and beyond to Bondi. It was certainly every bit as democratic, given that it was free and open to all comers, rich or poor, black or white, young or old, 365 days a year – rain or shine.

I, of course, could never admit it, but from that day on I decided to attend church on Saturdays not Sundays. Rather than sit on a pew, I swim in a lane. During the races, I'm well aware that I look like a sea elephant having a fit (particularly during the medley), but to me it's as close as I get to communion. And I haven't got to pretend to take part.

Advance
Australia Fair

A number of my friends and colleagues in the UK can't accept my love for Australia.

It's not just that they don't understand it – they don't *agree* with it.

My passion for the place somehow offends them.

Once it became clear that my feelings weren't a passing infatuation and that I intended to stay for good, the arguments – subtle and not so subtle – started to come out.

Leaving aside the lazy 'it's a crappy ex-prison we've no longer got a use for' prejudice of the morons who have never even been here, there were basically three distinct arguments employed to try to make me change my mind and return to the northern hemisphere.

The first was the 'you'll get bored of the beach, Nige' argument. This centred around the belief that my feeling smitten was simply the product of suddenly being in a sunny country after having spent the previous three decades in a rainy one. It followed that once the novelty passed and I was no longer enamoured of the beach lifestyle, I would take off my rose-tinted glasses and finally be able to see the country for the cultureless ex-colony that it was.

Well, it's now been six years and quite the opposite has happened. Not only have I not become bored of the 'beach lifestyle', I've immersed myself steadily deeper into it with every passing year. When I was training for my first rough-water ocean swim, my Pommy disbelievers didn't believe I would do it. Could do it, more to the point. When I duly completed one (albeit extremely slowly), they commented that now I had successfully scratched the itch and ticked off this particular goal, I would never do another one. Again, they were wide of the mark – I'm currently up to sixteen completed races and am loving each new one every bit as much as the first.

Not only that, I also entered, trained for and passed my Bronze Medallion exam, qualifying as a lifesaver. Unbelievably, for a former fat, non-swimming Pom, I now occasionally don the red and yellow *Baywatch* gear and patrol my local beach. My first patrol was on Boxing Day 2006 and, mercifully, it was incident-free – apart, that is, from being caught by my mum slacking off in the local cafe drinking a coffee. 'Back of beach patrol duties,' I called it.

As well as being laughable, the 'you'll get sick of the beach' argument is inherently flawed. You see, while I love Australia's beaches and its weather, I'm not committed to living in Australia for that reason alone. Much as some Brits I know scoff at my views, I want to live here *because* of the culture. I don't find Australia cultureless – I find it abundantly, joyously cultureful. What I'm about to say isn't a value judgement. I'm very happy that we are all different and like different things. What I'm about to say is merely a personal point of view.

I prefer Australian culture to British culture.

That doesn't mean I don't like Britain, British people or British culture.

I do.

(In fact, keep it to yourself, but to this day I still can't stop myself screaming for the British Lions.)

It's just that I prefer Australian culture. I'm British by birth, Australian by choice – and happy with both.

I'd still want to live here if it was rainy every day, not sunny. I've come to realise that Australia has a polarising effect on a number of people – not just Little Englanders. On a recent business trip to Singapore, I was shocked to learn that many Singaporeans commonly and openly refer to Australians as the 'white trash of Asia'. Everyone's got the right to their own opinion, I suppose. Me, I adore the 'no worries' vibe, the friendliness, the lack of class structure, the notion of giving everyone a fair go, the collective desire to take the piss out of anyone who gets above themselves and starts putting on airs, the inspirational heroism of Aussies throughout history, the mateship, the diversity, the pulling together in hard times, the natural love of an underdog, the Aussie battlers who keep their heads down and uncomplainingly get on with it through thick and thin, the sense of being a young, small nation that has to put up with so much patronising sentiment yet still retains a calm inner belief in the incredibly valuable and important role it has to play in this world. And yes, I love the sport – and the love of sport.

So all in all, it would be fair to say the 'you'll get bored of the beach' argument cuts no ice with me.

My UK doubters' second attempt fares little better but is worth examining because it reveals an interesting mindset. This particular 'anti-living in Australia' argument can be summarised as the 'it's just so damn far away' objection.

My natural response to this is, 'Far away from what?' It is obviously geographically true that Bronte is a very long way away from New York. It's equally true, however, that it is extremely close to Bronte Beach.

It just depends on what you view as the centre of the world. Or, more accurately, the centre of *your* world. I know many who haven't yet made this subtle distinction. If the only way you have of deciding where the epicentre lies is by looking at where society in general's most important hub is, then by definition you should never live anywhere but Manhattan Island – and the further you get from Manhattan, the more pointless and irrelevant the locale becomes.

For me, however, the epicentre of my world is Bronte Beach pool. And it follows from this that the further I get from there, the less attractive the location. Under my definition, New York is the place that is 'just so damn far away'. Lovely though it may be, it is unthinkably far from the main action for my taste. I feel a lot of people would be happier if they could define, or build, their own epicentre, rather than accept or try to adopt other people's. If you feel New York or London is the centre of your world, that's great – live there. If you don't but feel you somehow need to be within striking distance of what *other* people define as the centre, I humbly suggest you might be setting yourself up for a lifetime of missed opportunities.

I was recently having this very same self-serving conversation with a local friend who happens to share my belief about Bronte's central role in the universe. He is from Boston and extremely successful in business so doesn't speak from an anti-American or anti-commerce perspective. 'Being a long way from London or New York isn't a bad thing, it is a very good thing. No – a great thing,' he said as we buttered our Turkish toast and surveyed the surf. 'To my mind, Nigel, Bronte is not far away *enough*.'

Obviously, it is a matter of perspective, but the 'it's too far away' argument is as ineffective with me as the 'you'll get bored of the beach' approach.

Which leaves their third and final argument – the 'it's so economically insignificant' line of attack. Now, with the greatest of respect to all who live in this wonderful land, they are right. It *is* economically insignificant. In my previous CEO roles, it didn't matter how successful I was in running the company. Even if I had quadrupled the size of the firms, they would still have represented four-fifths of fuck-all of the worldwide turnover of the international company they were a part of.

Yet, interestingly, both those international companies *loved* their Australian office and really valued its contribution. *Because they judged the worth of the office on other criteria than economic size.* They accepted the self-evident truth that the Australian company was never going to be the engine for revenue growth on a worldwide basis and focused instead on things such as the quality of the work we were doing, the quality of the people we were training, the new methods of operating that we were trying.

It is the same attitude I have towards the country as a whole. I willingly accept that however successful the Australian economy is, we will forever represent a tiny percentage of the globe's GDP. To equate that fact with overall insignificance, however, is a foolish and tragic mistake. I believe there are so many ways in which Australia could, and should, aspire to lead the world – rather than striving to be a pale me-too version of the US or UK.

There's a story of a conversation Bill Clinton had with Edward de Bono a couple of years ago, when they were both in Hong Kong. Bill asked Ed his opinion of what in an ideal world the perfect nation would look like. De Bono replied, 'It would have an ethnically diverse population of twenty to twenty-five million people. English would be the national language. It would be religiously and economically liberated, have a democratic form of government and a vigorous free press. I'd locate it somewhere along the Pacific Rim. It would have a young history and an optimistic outlook. And a generous climate that lent itself to encouraging all its people – rich or poor – to enjoy the wonderful free gifts nature has to offer.'

'Sounds wonderful,' Clinton wistfully remarked. 'What would you call it?' he asked.

'Oh, I wouldn't change its name,' de Bono replied. '"Australia" will do fine.'

I'm not saying Australia is perfect. It isn't. I'm not saying it hasn't had a troubled past. It has. All I'm saying is it has as good a chance, perhaps an even better chance, than any other country to lead the world. Not just in specific areas such as the environment, human rights, science, commerce and sport. But as an overall example of how a successful, free and modern society can happily and fruitfully function.

As with so many things, it comes down to a matter of leadership, I suppose – an area where, sadly, Australia hasn't always led the world. Call me a misty-eyed romantic, but I feel that with the right inspirational and visionary leadership, Australia could become a beacon of hope for the future of mankind. I love the country as it is, but even more, I love the idea of what the country *could be*.

This feeling stems not just from a specific love for the country and people, however. It is also a result of a general attitude. Over the last five years I have basically trained myself to try to look for the good in people and situations – however hard a search this can sometimes be. This doesn't mean denying the bad. It just means choosing to seek out, focus on and accentuate the good. I know people who are hardwired to look for and believe in the bad in people and situations. No surprise to report they can always find enough evidence to back up their world view. Thankfully, I've discovered the opposite is also true. If you look for and believe in the good you will usually be able to find enough evidence. Importantly, I think the latter world view *works better*. It fosters hope and encourages positive action. It also makes you a damn sight happier and nicer to be around. Maybe it's just dressed up selfishness but I've *chosen* to be positive. So all in all, if you combine my general philosophy with my specific infatuation, it would be fair to say I'm hopelessly biased about Australia.

Whatever the reasons behind my views, Kate tells me I can get embarrassingly carried away by my love of the country (mortifyingly, I wept during my citizenship ceremony), so it was with some relief that on a recent run in Centennial Park, I noticed that I'm not alone in my views – and, indeed, that my views aren't in any way new. There's a rotunda in the park called Federation Pavilion. It was built to celebrate Australia's bicentenary, its circular shape a symbol of unity.

On the outside of the building, there's an inscription that runs the entire way around the top of the wall – 'Mammon or Millennial Eden'.

This is a paraphrase of the question posed in Bernard O'Dowd's poem 'Australia':

A new demesne for Mammon to infest?
Or lurks Millennial Eden 'neath your face?

Again, I'm no lover of or expert on poetry, but I take this quote to be asking everyone – including a jogger happening to run by – whether Australia's future will be tied purely to material wealth or, instead, to the pursuit of slightly higher ideals.

Not a bad question to ponder, if you have a minute . . .

Fiscally Underwhelmed

So where have I ended up?

It's been more than a year since my second step back from the corporate world. More than enough time to take stock and review matters.

Well, for a start, Kate was right about the effect my career decision would have on our domestic life. There have been a number of money-based arguments. And, indeed, there have been a few rows about trivial stuff, such as her refusal to buy homebrand shampoo rather than the expensive stuff. The kids still haven't got curtains in their bedrooms, either. Given that they've survived the entire winter without them, it is possible that they will *never* get them now because, putting it bluntly, the money is running out. The family's finances are right royally rooted. And I can't see things changing in a hurry. I worked out a few weeks ago that I would have to sell precisely six copies of both of my books to every single man, woman and child in Australia to make a living from my writing. Something that not even my mother thinks is likely to happen.

If we accept for a moment that I'm not going to be able to convince the entire Australian population to buy six copies of the same book, however hard I try, the only other way to make money from my writing is to crack America. Imagine my euphoric delight, then, when earlier this year my agent called to tell me that my first book, *Fat, Forty and Fired*, had been picked up by an American publisher.

It was a dream come true.

'Kate!' I yelled from the kitchen. 'The Yanks love *Fat, Forty and Fired*. They want to launch it in hardback this July!'

'That's fabulous, sweetheart,' she replied.

'Dead right it is. Look out, Oprah, here I come! Do you think I should do Letterman or Leno? Or can you do both?' I only half-jokingly asked.

'Steady on, Nige, don't get your hopes up too soon. There's a difference between being published and being a bestseller,' she cautioned.

'Screw that! Dan Brown better watch his arse – there's a new sheriff coming to town.'

The kids were almost as excited as I was.

'Does this mean we'll get to meet the queen of America?' Eve asked.

'They haven't got a queen, stupid. It's a king,' Grace corrected her sister.

'Will I be able to visit *The Simpsons*' set?' Alex asked.

'What about Borat?' Harry added.

My mind reeled as I wondered how on earth my eight-year-old knew about Borat, let alone wanted to meet him. Nevertheless, not wanting to confuse matters with anything as boring as the truth, and without telling an actual lie, I let them believe that their dad was indeed going to single-handedly conquer the USA and, in the process, if not rub shoulders with Borat, then at the very least take tea with the king and queen of America.

It would be fair to say that a lot was riding on the American launch beyond my ego. This was a route to maintaining the new life I had embarked upon all those months ago. I knew that if something dramatic didn't happen soon, I would have to start thinking about re-re-entering the corporate world. Something I wasn't totally averse to but, then again, something I didn't want to do just yet.

It was a memorable moment therefore when, having given it a few weeks for the book to 'take off up the charts', I announced to the family after dinner that I was going to the spare room to 'check the book's position on the American bestseller list'. I felt slightly sick with excitement as I turned on my computer and logged on to amazon.com. A quick click of the mouse and a scroll down to the bottom of the page revealed that *Fat, Forty and Fired* was . . . 795,000th in the rankings.

Not 'top ten', not 'top 100', not 'top anything' really – just 795,000th. It was barely in the top *million* for fuck's sake. No curtains in the kids' bedrooms for a while yet then.

Thing is, in that instant when I stared at the computer screen in disbelief at all the noughts after the '795', I realised that I had a choice – be devastated at high hopes cruelly dashed and bitterly play the blame game, or count my blessings that it got published overseas in the first place. I wouldn't have believed it if you'd told me this a few years ago, but choosing the latter response actually worked. Worked just as well, in fact, as choosing the former option would have done. Choosing to be unhappy is equally effective. Trouble is, it means you end up unhappy. The facts are going to stay the same no matter what – the only thing you can change is your reaction to them. In most cases, it strikes me as an altogether more healthy decision to choose the happiness option. Truth be told, looked at with a bit of perspective, 795,000th is actually rather funny. Fiscally underwhelming . . . but funny all the same.

This incident leads me to a final observation. It stems from the realisation that despite having failed to topple Dan Brown from his throne, and the rather pressing monetary reality of our situation, I've never been happier. That's not to say I don't have my off days, or to deny that I can be a right miserable bastard at times, but on the whole I am really, genuinely happy. I'm not saying I'm happy *because* we now face more money issues than we used to, but I am saying I agree with philosopher Bertrand Russell's belief that 'to be without some of the things you want is an indispensable part of happiness'. Just as I believe that achieving balance is not about having it all, I've come to believe that being happy isn't about having it all, either.

A number of self-help gurus maintain that 'happiness isn't a destination, it's a journey'. It's a nice line, but I don't agree – I don't think happiness is a journey; my observation is that it is a *choice*.

For the majority living in a prosperous liberal democracy like Australia, the reality of modern-day life demands of people that they be responsible for making their own happiness. Or at least it should. Leave aside those who have genuine problems for a moment – for most of us, if you are unhappy in this society in this day and age, you have to consider the possibility that the problem lies with you rather than with the conditions that surround you. I know from my own personal experience that it is far easier to look around and blame other people and circumstances for your melancholy, but some good old-fashioned honest reflection made me realise that I have a simple choice: to make the best of the hand life deals me or to moan about it. I know people who have unimaginable wealth and privilege and are as permanently miserable as a wet weekend. I also know others who face enormous challenges and are some of the happiest people I've ever met.

It's very important to stress that I'm not arguing for Pollyannaish denial here, or urging anyone to join some happy-clappy cult. There are a number of 'experts' in this field who to my mind are guilty of hideously exaggerating what is achievable. One such expert has even written a bestseller called (and I'm not making this up) *You Can Be Happy No Matter What*. No matter what? Umm . . . not so sure about that. I don't think it is possible to be happy all the time. Nor wise to expect to be. Certain events and tragedies are intrinsically awful and, however you look at them, not the stuff of happiness. I don't think we should try to be happy about how AIDS is ravaging certain parts of Africa, or the devastation that is being inflicted on innocent families in war-torn regions. On a personal level, I don't want to be told I can be happy about my dad's condition, either. Sure, I can stop myself from wallowing in misery and self-pity. I can strive to gain perspective and look for the things I can do to make the situation better. But 'happy'? No.

Having said the above, I *do* think that you can train yourself to intelligently, pragmatically and consistently look on the bright side in most of day-to-day life. Crises and tragedies aside for a moment, I believe we can *decide* to be happy in everyday life. More than that, my observation is that for many of us, this decision can be one of the most important we will ever make. If we put just a fraction of the effort we spend on trying to change our circumstances into changing our attitude, we can transform our lives – literally overnight.

So, after a year's reflection as a very short man, this is where I have rather unremarkably ended up – in agreement with Abraham Lincoln's disarmingly simple yet profound remark that 'people are just about as happy as they make up their minds to be'. I've especially taken the 'as happy' bit to heart. As I've come to believe that happiness is a state of mind not a set of circumstances, I've also come to raise my sights. I don't want to settle for being averagely happy – life's too short. I'm shooting for ecstatic, infectious joy. I now strive to make up my mind on a daily basis to try not just to be happy with circumstances, whatever they are, but to be *delighted* with them.

Not that I wouldn't mind being a bit taller, however . . .

Acknowledgements

First I would like to acknowledge the remarkable Jude McGee. I feel blessed to have the privilege of such a wonderful editor and friend.

Next love, affection and heartfelt thanks to the family and friends in this fabulous country and beyond who have shown me such kindness throughout the writing and publishing process.

Among the many people to whom I am indebted I wish to express particular thanks to Tara Wynne, Peter Giutronich, Bill Ford, Tim Castree, Pippa Masson, Paul Donovan, Dani Simonds, Patrick Gallagher, Karen Williams, Renee Senogles, Darian Causby, Joanne Holliman, Fiona Daniels, Lou Johnson, Elissa Baillie,

Caitlin Withey and the entire Allen & Unwin sales team.

Special thanks also go to all the *Fat, Forty and Fired* readers who have written with messages of encouragement and support. It means the world to me.

Above all, and as always, my fathomless gratitude to my dear wife, Kate. This book would not exist without her.

www.nigelmarsh.com